The Power of
Connected Marketing

The Power of Connected Marketing

3 of the World's Leading Marketing Experts reveal their proven Online, Offline & In-store Strategies to grow your Business and Dominate your marketplace.

Troy Spring | Glenn Pasch | Tracy Myers

To order additional copies of this book, contact:
Xlibris
1-888-795-4274
www.Xlibris.com
Orders@Xlibris.com
699386

CONTENTS

"The first time I was provoked to think differently about Marketing was reading Seth Godin in Fast Company Magazine in the late '90s. Seth said things like **'whatever you SELL is BORING! Insurance is BORING—Advertising is BORING—it's all BORING...' UNLESS, you or I make it REMARKABLE in the eyes of the customer!** This book is the next level of PROVOKING you to THINK DIFFERENTLY about something you may already (think you) know a lot about. There is an overload of BORING MARKETING today in the most sophisticated marketplace the world has ever known. Following in the swath cut by Ogilvy, Kennedy, Godin and a few others, what Tracy, Glenn and Troy have done here is to take the time to PROVOKE/TEACH others to BECOMING REMARKABLE when it comes to selling and marketing in this NOW ECONOMY. This book means BUSINESS!"

-Michael York: Business Consultant/CEO/Author

"The irony of "The Power of Connected Marketing" is that by reading it, your marketing ROI will never be unconnected again. Glenn, Troy, and Tracy reveal how you can unify your business' marketing efforts to produce efficient marketing budgets that create results that dominate your market."

-Michael Cirillo: Author, Podcaster, Owner Dealer Flex

"Today's marketing is almost 100% data driven, especially online! Do you know how to measure it? Do you have the courage to discuss it?

A basic marketing plan should show me what you're going to do, how you're going to do it, and how you're going to track the results to the bottom line. "The Power of Connected Marketing" makes sense. Everyone must be accountable and transparent in today's world! The customer is changing faster then ever before, shouldn't your marketing approach? Market to where your customers will be, not to where they are!"

**-Sean Stapleton: Former VP of Sales
and Marketing, Vin Solutions**

"The times, they have a'changed. In case you haven't noticed, people don't even call before visiting anymore and you can be sure they're comparing you, not just to the option next door, but also to the best alternative anywhere in the world. Glenn, Troy and Tracy's book is simply the best guide I can think of for anyone assembling, expanding or improving their sales and marketing organization in the digital / social age."

-Alberto Molina: CEO of SureTech

Acknowledgements

Glenn Pasch:

To my parents Jim and Frances first and foremost for the example you have set.

To my brother Brian who has been a great brother, leader and business partner. Keep doing what you do.

To my team at PCG. Thanks for delivering excellence in all you do for our company, our clients and the industry.

To my sons William and Alex who make me laugh and smile every day. I am so proud of you both.

Lastly, to my wife Mayra, simply put, the best thing that has ever happened to me. Period.

To my fellow authors Troy Spring and Tracy Myers. Thanks for including me on this crazy project. I have learned from you both and appreciate your friendships.

Troy Spring:

To my wife Brittany who supports every crazy idea I have in life with a smile on her face.

To my children, whom I work so hard to set an example for.

To the long list of clients, industry friends, including Glenn Pasch and Tracy Myers who have supported my career and philosophies over the years.

And to the talented and passionate team at Dealer World who I am honored to work with everyday.

Tracy Myers:

Many thanks to my Lord and Savior Jesus Christ for all of His blessings. Through Him, all things are possible.

Much love to my amazing wife, Lorna, for being my best friend.

To Presley and Maddie. My heart...my children. Always remember that I love you more.

To my mom, dad and grandparents: I'm grateful that you led me down the right path but never left me alone and for always giving me a swift kick in the behind when I needed it. I'm forever grateful and I love you.

To all of my Teammates at Frank Myers Auto Maxx, WrestleCade Entertainment, AML Wrestling and America's Most Liked Dealer Services: I appreciate what all of you do and THANK YOU is not enough. Let's keep doing what we do!

To my co-authors Troy Spring and Glenn Pasch: thank you for trusting in me to contribute to this book. I admire you both and appreciate your friendship.

Speaking of friends, thank you for your friendship even though I'm not a good friend. However, I'm still learning. Much peace and love.

Marketing Silos Are Killing Your Business

For the purpose of this book, we will refer to "traditional marketing" (TV, radio, print, mail) as *offline* and digital marketing efforts (website, SEO, SEM social media, digital advertising) as *online*. We will then refer to anything you do in your brick-and-mortar location as *on-site* marketing.

Too often we hear business leaders and agencies talking about their marketing efforts in terms of "traditional" marketing and "digital" marketing. What this classification has done is to create different messages and confusion for both parties because one team (or silo) does not know what the other is doing. Our goal with this book is to change the marketing silo mentality in businesses and to allow people to focus on their marketing efforts as a whole or connected effort.

For example, I spoke to a digital marketing manager for a midsize automotive dealer group one day. We were discussing how to reallocate some of his marketing dollars, and immediately the marketing silo language came out of his mouth. We were discussing the benefits of video preroll and possibly moving some of his marketing budget from cable TV over to this online video marketing product. When I asked him what cable spots he was running and how often they were running, he said that he did not know. He was not privy to that.

This brief exchange reinforced a symptom of marketing in general but especially in the automotive vertical. I have seen, in my time as CEO of PCG, a great many unconnected marketing efforts because offline marketing is not in tune with online efforts. Too many times marketing silos rule decisions. I believe this was an outgrowth of leadership having an ad agency that handled all their marketing needs previously, and as digital marketing began to grow, it was not something this ad agency could handle. This led to hiring a new agency to market online or, worse, just getting products and spending money without having a strategic partner to guide this marketing spend. Thus, two marketing silos were created; and thus, no one exchanged information.

The goal of this book is to change this dialogue and get people to focus on connected marketing efforts, by looking at the customer journey from offline, to online, to in-store or anywhere the customer connects to your message.

An industry expert said, "What is the goal of almost all of your offline marketing today? To drive the viewer to your website where you have all of your online marketing efforts. So if both of your marketing teams are not communicating, then between offline and online teams, how will that union work?"

I agree. As I said to this manager, where is the "traditional" marketing silo sending the clicks? What is the message they are sharing? If it is not connected with your online efforts, then the customer will receive a disjointed experience, and you will lose potential sales.

What needs to happen beginning today is that all marketing partners have to have a seat at the connected marketing table.

What should a connected marketing process look like? Here are a few quick ideas.

- Think of the shopper's path from stimulus (offline marketing) and how/where it will drive these interested people online (website, research, etc.).
- Make sure messaging of all marketing efforts match in color and feel.
- Make sure that marketing can track the interaction back to the offline asset if offline marketing efforts are sending individuals to a specific page on the website or using a specific phone number to contact the business.
- Leadership has to treat both groups as a part of the whole marketing message. So if the path is offline (TV, radio, print) to online (website, etc.) to on-site (banners, signs, posters), then you have a consistent path for the consumer to follow in order to do business with you.

Once we have our offline team and online team at the table, we have to invite a third: on-site marketing.

What do I mean by on-site marketing? What is in your brick-and-mortar store that continues the marketing effort for your customer? Let's take that journey.

- The offline team has created a great TV spot highlighting a special offer your business is providing for a holiday weekend. They reach out to the online team to explain the ad/message and ask them what website URL they should use in the spot to send the traffic to the right place.
- The digital team then creates a special landing page highlighting the offer with a strong call to action. The key is that the visual of the ad matches what they saw on TV. The digital team then continues by promoting the campaign on the website and online. They may do it through blog content, social media, as well as using a remarketing banner and video preroll campaign on YouTube. The goal is to engage the customer and get them to contact the dealership.

We know through different research projects that 70% of customers do not contact the company before coming in. For those who call or e-mail, the staff on-site needs to make sure that those responding are up to date on the promotion. What happens, though, when the customer just walks in? This is now where on-site marketing comes into play.

When the customer enters the building, they need to see visual stimulus that confirms this is the right location. Are there signs and banner stands showing the promotion that they saw online? Are there table tents or flyers confirming that this is indeed the location that marketed that offer?

Use on-site marketing tools to finish your marketing journey. If you do not, then you run the risk that the customer is unsure if they are in the right location and leave.

Not having your three teams to the table, working in unison is no longer an option. Without a strong three-headed solution, the customer journey is disrupted. In this very competitive marketplace, those who make it easy for the customer to find what they were looking for will win. Remember, silos will kill your business.

A word of caution. There is no straight line with Connected Marketing. Even though the book is written in sections do not think that this is the order you must follow. A customer may find you first online then they may receive a piece of mail you sent (offline) or drop into your location as they passed by and then went online. Having a Connected Marketing plan allows your consistent message to be where your customer is and allows them to interact with your company based on their desired path.

Let's dive into Online Media first because people are spending so much time online to research their shopping needs.

Online Marketing by Glenn Pasch

Fact: 80% to 90% of shoppers go online before contacting a business.

Fact: A company's online presence is now their most important marketing initiative.

Fact: Digital marketing spending is now increasing as a portion of total marketing budgets.

Fact: Business owners dread conversations about digital marketing.

SEO, SEM, video preroll, AdWords analytics, optimization, rich snippets, and the names go on and on. These send a chill down the spines of many business owners. To many, it is like taking medicine. You know you have to take it, that it will help you in the long run, but you are sure it is going to taste bad.

I have found that the fear of engaging with digital marketing causes business owners to feel that they have to change the way they run their business, and that in turn makes them feel obsolete.

In my mind, online marketing is a pretty simple concept. It may take time and some self-education to master techniques, but never think that you cannot understand it. The goal of online marketing is the same as any other marketing: getting customers to contact you. There are different tools and processes you will need to understand, but once you connect your online marketing, with offline and in-store marketing, you will see how easy it is.

I have put together some examples in this graphic. What this graphic shows is how tools and strategies that were used in the past have a counterpart in today's online medium. For example, in the past, a company may have advertised in the Yellow Pages. Today, they would use Google My Business (Google +).

Understanding the Digital Parallels

- Television = Youtube or Hulu or Netflix
- Valpak Coupons = Groupon
- Sears Catalog = Amazon
- TV Ads = Online Video Pre-Roll Ads
- Local Newspaper Ads = Facebook Ads
- Six o'clock news = Twitter
- Life Magazine = Pinterest
- Radio Station = Pandora
- Hanging Out With Friends = Facebook
- Encyclopedia = Wikipedia
- International Calling Card = Skype
- Rolodex = LinkedIn
- Billboard Advertising = Display Advertising
- Yellow Pages = Google My Business
- Storefront = Website
- Business Card Organizers =CRM
- Beepers = Text Messaging
- Consumer Reports Magazine = Online Peer Reviews
- Postcards = Instagram

Let me share a story. My company was teaching a digital marketing workshop to a group of automotive dealers. We were discussing video preroll, which are the short video advertisements that are seen before you watch videos online. An older gentleman who is a very successful dealer pulled me aside to ask me more about video preroll. I took the time to ask him if he used cable TV to run ads. He said, "Yes, because people watch cable."

I said to him, "Video pre-roll is the way to show your ads to the people who watch their TV or video online. Can you see how this could be effective?"

He smiled and, within minutes, was telling everyone he was going to do video preroll because I was the first person to make him understand what it was in terms he understood. That to me is what I hope you will take away from this section. Empowering you to bridge the gap from past to present, not intimidate or confuse.

But before we go down this road, let's take a step back.

When I was young, I used to think that people lived in the television, that somewhere inside that box, when I changed programs, people had to scurry around and get in front of the screen and perform for me. I am sure many of us thought the same thing when we were young.

A few years ago a popular animated movie used this concept to perfection using video games as the basis for the story. The film takes place in a video arcade, and when the arcade is closed at night, the characters in the games come to life as if performing in the game was their day job. We see them interact with one another and even go home for the night just as we do each day. The next day, back to work, so when the arcade was open and someone put money into the machine, they all got into place and performed their part.

My point is this, this imagery is a perfect way for me to help you understand online marketing and how the search engines work. If we could imagine that inside our computers, when we type in a search query, there are little characters whose job it is to search through the Internet records and bring out relevant pieces of content to show the search engine master. The search engine master's job is to review each of these submissions and then decide in terms of relevancy which piece goes in which order to fill the spots on page 1 that you will see. We know that there are more search pages shown than the first page, but for our discussion of marketing, page 1 is what matters.

If we embrace this imagery, then what our job as marketers should be is to learn what we need to do to make our content more relevant. If we do, then the search engine master moves us up higher on the list and eventually into the first spot. Now a word of caution. I can see the excitement on your faces. You cannot show up in the first spot on page 1 of search engines for every phrase that comes into your mind. Your goal is to have your content be relevant for your name, the service, or product you provide and where you do business.

When I say content, I mean everything someone can find about you online. Websites, blogs, articles, videos, business listings, social media profiles, forums, and the list goes on and on. Much of this content you should contribute yourself. This is what we will focus on first.

Before we move further into this book, let's talk about what this section is and what it is not. My goal is to help you understand the concepts of online marketing, what you should be doing at a high level, and to inspire you to ask better questions of your marketing partners. It is not going to be a deep dive into the how-to of these topics.

There are many other good books or websites out there for you to explore. In our reference section at the end, we will list other resources you can utilize to increase your education.

Here is a summary of what we will discuss in this section.

1. The Busy Marketplace and Online Marketing
2. Your Online "why buy from me?" Message
3. I Have a Website: Now What?
4. Tools You Need (SEO/SEM/Video/Display/Content)
5. Social Media: A Quick Thought
6. Mobile Is the Future
7. The Reputation Marketing and Customer Testimonials
8. Picking the Right Vendor Partner: What You Need to Ask
9. Budgeting, Reporting, and Accountability
10. The On-Demand Economy

The Busy Marketplace
and Online Marketing

I have a question for the reader. How did you find out about this book? My guess would be that someone recommended it to you *online* or you saw a marketing campaign: *online* or maybe social media—*online*.

Are you seeing a pattern? Online is where consumers are sharing information.

There are tons of statistics that I could overwhelm you with about today's online shopper, but here are a few of the most important that happened every minute in 2015: (statistics from an inforgraphic produced by Domo.com)

- 4 million search queries a minute on Google
- Facebook users share 4,166,667 posts
- You Tube uploads 300 hours of new video
- Twitter users tweet 347,222 times
- Instagram users like 1,736,111 photos

Before you close the book and think how will your content have a chance to stand out in this ever-growing ocean of content, I think it will be more effective to think of search engines from your personal perspective.

When you want information on pretty much any topic, what do you do? You Google it. (Or Bing it. Doesn't sound as cool, though). When you want to find a location or a product, what do you do? You Google it. Or use an APP on your mobile device that will show you content that you will read or watch. Our smartphones are near us at all times, almost as an extension of our arms. So with all of this content out there, all of these people searching, I want us to agree that your business will be in this big swarm of information on the web, and online marketing is used to help you or your company stand out.

But, Glenn, how can we do it? Is there a secret?

I am sorry to say there is no special sauce that the search engines have shared, although there are many who claim to have the keys to the search engines. Beware of these Gurus. (*We will discuss choosing a vendor partner later in this section*.) One thing that we need to remember when discussing online marketing is that we all are using someone else's product to advertise our business online: the search engines and advertising platforms are owned by companies. We as marketers do not control them. So we cannot just "get it fixed" or call Google customer support and instantly get something moved up on page 1.

What many good marketers (and you the reader) should focus on is working to understand what Google or search engines expect from you as a user of their product.

This knowledge will help to optimize your content so that the Search Engine Master is pleased. We also have to commit consistent resources to online marketing each month. This is not a one-time marketing play. You have to work at it every month.

So let's begin the journey into the realm of online marketing by creating our foundation.

Why Buy from Me?

This is the foundation upon which every future marketing effort or strategy will be built. Unless you are providing such a unique product or service that you dominate your market without competition, then you are competing for attention online.

Let's understand why the "why buy from me" is the foundation of your success.

Let me use some of my clients from the automotive industry as an example. Dealers are coming to realize that as important as their vehicles are to consumers, they also understand that consumers can purchase the same vehicle in a variety of locations.

Once a consumer decides on a vehicle, they will now begin their research on which dealership to purchase the car from. This same two-pronged search strategy applies to many businesses.

Online marketing strategies will help to get your listing into someone's search results, but you need to present a great reason for them to click further and ultimately do business with you. Having a clearly laid out "why buy" message online will peak the customer's interest and earn you the opportunity to interact with them. I can hear some of you saying many consumers just want a low price. I agree in part because no one wants to feel like they overpaid, but many consumers are willing to pay for a great experience or for the comfort of knowing they will be taken care of.

So what is your message? Why should I do business with you? If you cannot tell me, then let's figure it out. If you can, before we move forward, let me ask you something important. Could your competitor say the same thing you are claiming? Hmmm.

Let's take a moment to complete the following exercise.

Take out a blank piece of paper, or if you have a team of people who will participate in the exercise, gather them in a room and have a whiteboard or a large piece of paper on an easel that they can all see.

Have everyone share their reasons why consumers should do business with you. Do not edit your answers; just write them down. I am sure a list will come together pretty fast.

Take a moment to review all of the responses so that no answers are repetitive or the group thinks they missed anything.

Once this list is completed, ask those present to cross out any of the claims that your competitor could say. Things like "provides value," "customer focused," "fair deals," or even "fifty years in Town" can be said by a competitor. Be fair but hard with your crossing off of these claims. You are building a solid foundation for all of your marketing but especially online.

Once you have your few unique marketing points, this is where you begin. This is now the foundation that you will build your marketing message and strategy upon. Without this, you will have a ten-story building that is rocky and potentially will collapse upon itself.

NOTE: Test out your message on a few close friends to see if they agree that this is how they think of you or your business.

Great. We have our "why buy from me" message, and we are using it effectively in our offline marketing (Troy's chapter). Next step is to understand how to implement this message in your online marketing.

FACT: All of your offline marketing is leading people to look for you online.

Let me repeat that for emphasis because it is one of the most important points of this section.

<u>All of your offline marketing is leading people to look for you online.</u>

Even if it is to confirm your location, consumers are doing what they always do when they need information: grabbing their phone, tablet, or computer and begin typing away. Off our little characters go into the Internet to search for relevant content to show to the search engine master (remember him), and hopefully, you have made the top 10 and, more importantly, top 3 spots on page 1 for that search query.

We will go into more detail later about connecting your marketing across these three areas (offline, online and on-site), but a word of caution right from the beginning. Make sure that whoever is creating your offline materials understands where to send the customers online. Every piece of offline marketing now contains your website. You will need to direct them to where you want this consumer to go on your website to create a great experience. Too much money can be wasted by allowing those not trained in online marketing to direct this customer traffic to your website.

I Have a Website. Now What?

I included this title because I have heard it said by many small business owners and even some large businesses as well. "Won't just having a website be enough?"

I am sorry to say, but no, it is not.

Your website is your brick-and-mortar location online. For some businesses, it is the link between research and coming to your physical location. For some types of companies, this is the only place where business gets done.

First let's focus on the user experience before getting too technical. So what does your website need?

1. Easy to understand: what you do, what services and products you offer.
2. It should be very clear why I should do business with you.
3. Photos of staff.
4. Blog or educational content.
5. Social sharing icons
6. Clear call to actions.
7. Easy to find contact information and location (if applicable).
8. Quality of content and level of understanding should be easy to read.

9. It should contain reviews from third party and/or reviews from your customers.
10. It should contain videos because 40% of people like to watch videos more than read.

We can add more to this list later, but these things, I think, are a good place to begin. At first glance, you may feel that many of these are in place already, and that is a good thing. I would recommend reviewing your site with this list next to you to make sure.

If you are missing any of these, then put it on your list to address right away. Your website is a representation of your business. It is not a static location where once you place your information, nothing changes. You have to make sure it is constantly up to date.

So how do we become relevant? Remember this is not a specific deep dive into how to do each of these things I will mention, but I will speak at a high level on what has to happen. This should spur conversations with your vendor providers or challenge you to get further education to make these things happen.

Here are three tips to make it easier for consumers to find your content on your website:

Tip: Make sure your agency or digital marketing partner has set up your website metadata (techy-type word) and descriptions to let the search engines know what your site is relevant for. The same goes for each page of your site. It should have a page title and description that describes what the page is about. As the search engines crawl over your site, if you tell them the page is one thing with the title and then the content has nothing to do with the title, then the relevancy of the page is diminished and will hurt your site in search.

Think of when you wrote a paper for English class. You have a title for your paper, a summary of what you were going to share and then the content. If any of this did not match, for example the content did not relate to the title, then you received a lower grade. Same goes for the pages on your website.

Tip: Watch the number of drop downs on your navigation bar. I see some cases where when I click on the "About Us" navigation tab, there are eight to ten things on the drop down. (Meet staff, about us, hours, maps, testimonials, videos, etc.). I can understand how it limits the number of tabs, but it makes it hard for me to find what I am looking for. This goes against making it easy for your customers to find your content.

Tip: Maybe think of converting some of your categories or services into buttons on the site so it is easy to find this information. In the example below, PCG takes a drop-down menu and converts it into an easy-to-use experience for their visitors. When you click on the icon, it takes you to a specific page about that service.

Let's take a moment to look at some of the pages on my company's websites:

1. Easy to understand what you do, what services and products you offer. **CHECK**
2. It should be very clear why I should do business with you. **CHECK**
3. Photos of staff. **CHECK**
4. Blog or educational content. **CHECK**
5. Social sharing icons. **CHECK**
6. Clear call to actions. **CHECK**
7. Easy to find contact information and location (if applicable). **CHECK**
8. Quality of content and level of understanding should be easy to read. **CHECK**
9. It should contain reviews from third party and/or reviews from your customers. **CHECK**
10. It should contain videos because 40% of people like to watch videos more than read. **CHECK**

PCG

REAL PEOPLE ⌄   REAL STRATEGIES ⌄   REAL RESULTS ⌄   RESOURCES   BLOG   CONTACT   Q

STAY IN TOUCH

But only if you want the latest news in digital marketing

SIGN UP FOR OUR NEWSLETTER

Real People. Real Strategies. Real Results.

Basically, we're a team of individuals working towards one common goal: providing our clients with a customized, personal, and unparalleled digital experience. Our NJ digital marketing company is composed of real people from all walks of life collaborating and innovating daily to be the best in the internet marketing business—and that's exactly what we are.

DIGITAL MARKETING SOLUTIONS

Content Creation

People have a right to know how amazing your business is. Let our wordsmiths spread the word.

SEO

Your search is over. Join us on Page One.

Website Design

What does your website say about you? All the right things when you let us take care of it.

Social Media Branding

People are talking online. Let's get them talking about you.

Paid Search

Look what your target market just found – You. PPC and SEM that works.

Remarketing

That potential customer that got away? We can get them back for you.

WHAT'S NEW

SUBSCRIBE

Get the latest digital marketing news, tips and tricks sent directly to your inbox. CLICK HERE

CONTACT US

📍 446 Route 35 South, Building C
Eatontown, NJ 07724

📱 Phone:(888) 798-1195

LINKS

PCG Consulting Services
PCG Research
ROI-bot

To search type and hit enter

We work hard here at PCG Digital Marketing because
we want to foster solid relationships with our digital marketing
clients that lead to undeniable results.

We know our clients appreciate this dedication because they've told us so:

The responsiveness of PCG helps a great deal, as professional and appealing graphics are created quickly
and they manage the 'back-end' on our behalf. Driving this is an account manager who is easily reached
to provide advice and guidance on generating the best results.

PAUL LAPPAGE | ONLINE MARKETING MANAGER, LEGACY FORD

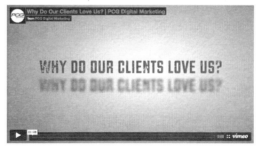

Each customer's needs are different, which is why our NJ-based agency builds internet marketing campaigns from the ground
up each time. This fresh approach helps us produce effective, measurable results for each client. As they say, "Seeing is
believing," so feel free to check out a few of the success stories in our collection of case studies.

VIEW OUR CASE STUDIES

Creating a Content Strategy

Now that we have shown examples of a website, one of the most important things you now need to focus on is a content strategy. This will help your site to be shown for your services when someone is searching in your area. In order to do that, new content has to be added regularly. The Internet is a growing thing that needs to be fed content and information. It is the information beast. If the little people who live in the computer need to go find information to show someone who puts in a search query, will the content you have online currently make your website relevant?

The common denominator for all content has to be that it is engaging and inspires consumers to contact you. As I mentioned, when I say content, it can mean a few different things. It could mean new pages on your site, updating your current pages, blogs, social media posts, videos, and banners.

You accomplish this by making sure much of the content is educational. This will position your company as the expert at what you do and will help to give consumers a reason to engage your services.

Examples of educational content:

1. Provide people with information on your services to educate them on why they need your service.
2. Explain the process of interacting with you.

3. Explain how your service saves them time or money or provides the solution.
4. Provide third-party articles about your industry.
5. Make the website a place for consumers to get information versus getting on your site and then having to leave to get an answer to a question that you should have answered.

Example 1: if you are car dealer and you provide vehicle service to drivers, why not create a series of videos focusing on the top 10 questions you receive about service.

- How often to change wiper blades?
- Why do we need the right tire pressure?
- How to add windshield washer fluid?
- What should I keep in the trunk for long trips?

Think of the ways you could share this content across the web and be seen as someone helping your customers and consumers.

Example 2: You are a carpet cleaning service. Types of content you could provide:

- Why you need to clean your carpet regularly?
- What kinds of bacteria live in carpets?
- What to do to get stains out?
- Best hypoallergenic carpets? Best carpets for pets?

The list goes on and on. You will be seen as the expert, providing useful educational information.

Example 3: If I am looking to remove an oil tank, do I know all of the ins and outs of what I have to do or what to look for? No. But if I come to a website that gives me the impression that you are the expert and willing to be open, transparent, and helpful, I am more willing to engage.

What if you had a list of 5 things to look for to help determine if you need your tank removed? What if you had a detailed process of the tank removal so it could help the consumer understand what the process entails?

There is some hesitation by some business owners to the idea of providing educational content. Their fear is that if they provide this content, then the consumer will not need their services. I disagree.

I subscribe to the rule of thirds. A third of the consumers will take the information and do it themselves. The good thing is they will return to your site for more information and may use your company if they run across a problem they cannot solve. You are now their expert for these services in their mind.

The second third of the people will take the info and do nothing with it. They have all good intentions, but in reality, they do not really want to implement a change.

The final third of the people will call you because they realize that they cannot handle the issue themselves. In their mind, by presenting this information, you must be the expert to take care of their problem.

Blogging

Blogging about topics is a great way to not only provide this type of educational content but also allows the voice of your business to shine through. Blogs could be short four-hundred-to five hundred-word articles on your site about your services or things going on in your area.

Don't think you have to be Hemingway to blog. Write in your own voice. Make sure it is not too technical and that it has a photo or image. That image will help grab attention. Also remember that a catchy title will also grab the eye of the reader.

I am asked about where to locate your blog. Should it be on your site, or should you create a separate blog website. My personal opinion is for a business, I prefer the blog to be on the site. This is more from a user experience first and foremost. I don't want people leaving my website to find information I should be providing.

There are some strategies that have the blog as a subdomain, which means it is a part of your site but not the main structure. Think of it as an addition to your house versus the original structure. To know if your blog is a subdomain or not, look at your URL structure. If it is blog.pcgdigitalmarketing versus pcgdigitalmarketing.com/blog, then it is a subdomain. I think the subdomain is better than a separate site, but still having your blog as a part of your main website is still the best.

Having a separate blog site could be a great idea if you are looking to be a more full- fledged content creator or you are dedicating this separate site to a specific product or service. It may seem like an easy thing to have another website, but it takes time and commitment. I would focus my time on my main site and my social profiles to build my strategy than having a multitude of micro-sites.

How often you should blog is up for debate. I recommend looking at who is able to contribute to this content. This is important because your strategy has to be consistent. It is better to start out slow and build up your amount of content versus putting out a great deal initially and then falling off pace. If you first committed to blog once a week, finding fifty-two topics is pretty easy. Ask yourself what are the top twenty questions you are asked the most about your services and how would you answer. That is half a year of blogging. There are also articles you have read about your industry that you could share or comment on. Remember, blogs are looking to be fun, informational, and engaging.

In my case, I have enough employees that we can blog five to six times a week. For my own personal website, I focus on writing one blog a week. I would love to increase that, and some weeks I do, but I always want to have at least one article.

If you are limiting your posting to once or twice a week, try to be consistent on the days you post. If you can be consistent, then your audience begins to expect your content and looks for it.

Video Content

The fun part of video content is that you can show off more of your company's personality in videos versus the written word. You can start by creating short videos based on some of the questions your written content answered. Don't worry about repeating ideas. Remember, many people like to watch content versus reading. If not, then why would all of the large news aggregation sites all have over 40% of their online content in video form. They would not be doing that if they had not done the relevant research to make sure it worked.

Here are a few videos that you should work on first if they apply.

1. Why buy from you
2. Video explaining process of using your service
3. Demonstration of your services or products
4. Customer testimonials
5. Fun things your company does
6. Charitable works

The list of video options is endless. Make sure that you work with your vendor to make sure these videos are optimized to work into your digital marketing strategy. You can use these videos on specific pages on your website, include them in blogs, share them on social media or even in your e-mail communication with customers.

For more in depth strategies, you could refer to my previous book *Selling Cars in the Digital Age.*

Lastly, banners, infographics, and photos can be used as content. Anything that can be shared that highlights your business or services is useful in your content strategy.

Note: This bears repeating. You content posting strategy should resemble more of the tortoise than the hare. You need to do a little each day versus a lot in a short period of time. People make the mistake to think they are too far behind, and it will take too long, so they try to make up time.

"If I do five videos this week, what if I post twenty? I can quadruple my impact!"

Not really. Search engines reward consistency. Long-term posting versus short-term volume. Search engines want to provide the best and most relevant content to their users. My advice is to always produce content thinking: "Is this going to help someone who is searching for my product or service?" This will help guide your decisions and help to anchor your content to your brand message.

Reminder: If you are posting content off your own website, make sure there are links back to the specific page on your site that is relevant to that service.

Linking

What do I mean when I say links? Think of a link as a connector or a finger pointing back to something that will give more detail to the topic. For instance, you may highlight the author of an article, which then links back to their LinkedIn profile. Maybe you have a specific offer for your product, and when someone clicks on the link, it goes to a specific page on your site describing the offer in more detail.

Links help the relevance of your website for certain terms. Part of your content strategy should be to strategically build the amount of these links pointing back to your site. Think of your time in high school. You got elected to student council by getting people to vote for you. Links do the same thing. If you have multiple links targeting the same keyword all pointing back to your site, then it begins to create more authority for your content; and in time, the search engines should show it in a higher position.

Let's go back to our oil tank removal company. Maybe someone on the staff was asked to write an article for an online forum focusing on the environment. The article was on "5 things to look for when removing your oil tank." Somewhere in the article was your company name (link it to your home page), then you have a sentence that says "oil tank removal in NJ," and you link this back to the page on your site, describing how you remove oil tanks in NJ. Limit the links to two to three per article. But by doing this in different areas, the page regarding "oil tank removal NJ" become more relevant for people searching this term in your area.

Note: A word of caution. Links must be of good quality. In the past, it was more about the number of links you had to impact your search visibility. The search engines changed this as they encountered people who abuse this practice.

Search engines have evolved now to where they can decide if links are of good quality or just spam. Be careful of companies promising to give you links if you pay them. This practice is wrong and will hurt your site. The search engines will penalize your website if they see it has a large number of mass produced links or bad strategic links. It is better to build good links over time. Again, think tortoise, not hare.

Remember the user experience when creating your linking strategy. When I click on your link, it should take me to where I need to go for the information you offered. Do not take me to a general page or your home page where I have to now figure out how to navigate and find the information. That will result in a bad user experience and frustrate your customers, thus reflective on your overall business image.

Keywords

Time to discuss keywords for a moment. Some people ask, "Which came first, content or keywords." To that I would answer, it depends.

So, Glenn, what are keywords?

Keywords are the terms that you would like to have your website show up for in search. Time for another word of caution. You cannot come up in the number 1 slot for every keyword combination you can think up. Your company is not relevant in every one of these searches. Focus initially on your company name, what your services and surrounding areas are, and build out the rest over time.

Keyword Search Self-Testing

Now, as a first test, type in the name of your business (ex: Glenn's oil tank removal), and your website should be in number 1 slot. Look at what else is coming up on page 1. You should see your social media profiles, business listings, review sites, videos, articles that mention your business, etc.

Look for any competitors who may be creating content using your name. Maybe they wrote a blog post or have a page on their site comparing their company to yours. This is a strategy companies use to be relevant in some of their competitors keywords.

Next, start thinking what would someone type if they did not know your company's name. Maybe "oil tank removal NJ" or "oil tank removal Eatontown." If that is where my business is or I have created relevant content around those words, my website should come up, or those pages on my site should come up.

Next, I begin to create a list of relevant keywords that I feel is important to my business. I do searches to see if I am visible for these queries, and if so, where is my website? I then begin to create a content strategy as well as an optimization strategy for my website.

There are many tools to help with keyword research (SEO Moz, Conductor Searchlight, Google AdWords Keyword Tool) as well as videos to help you decide on a keyword strategy. If your company has a website provider or an agency that is helping with your digital marketing strategies, you need to have conversations in regards to their keyword strategy.

Once you are dominating in these initial keywords, then you can begin the discussion of how to increase your reach, possibly conquering some of your competitors or different regions that you want to serve.

SEO (Search Engine Optimization)

These last few sections are set up to discuss SEO so you have an understanding of what this term means and how your content and keyword strategies work together.

Here is part of the definition from Wikipedia:

> **Search engine optimization (SEO)** is the process of affecting the visibility of a <u>website</u> or a <u>web page</u> in a <u>search engine</u>'s unpaid results - often referred to as "natural," "<u>organic</u>," or "earned" results. As an <u>Internet marketing</u> strategy, SEO considers how search engines work, what people search for, the actual search terms or keywords typed into search engines and which search engines are preferred by their targeted audience.
>
> Optimizing a website may involve editing its content, <u>HTML</u> and associated coding to both increase its relevance to specific keywords and to remove barriers to the <u>indexing activities</u> of search engines. Promoting a site to increase the number of <u>backlinks</u>, or inbound links, is another SEO tactic.

"Glenn, I am more confused after reading this. What does this mean in simple terms?"

Let me try to help you understand SEO at a simple level. We discussed before how your on page SEO should be looked at as you would a composition for English class. The title of your page tells the Search Engine Master what this will be about. If the description is matching, and helps explain why this page exists, then points are scored. If the content reinforces the title and descriptions, then your page is relevant.

I would recommend you reach out to your agency partner for help because it can be very confusing and also very expensive if SEO is not done correctly. If you website's SEO is not helping you be relevant in search, then you are losing opportunities to engage with potential customers.

So how can you quickly check? Go to any page and either right click on the page or look to your top toolbar on a Mac. Look for "View Source" it will show you the technical setup of the page.

DON'T freak out. I know it looks confusing but just look for the word <title> and read it. Then look for <description> and read that as well as the <keywords> that the page is targeting.

Let's look at our example of Glenn's Oil Change" company.

Title of a page targeting the city of Eatontown could be "Top Rated Oil Tank Removal Company Eatontown NJ"

Description should be something to the effect of, "Glenn's Oil Tank Removal Company is the top rated NJ oil tank removal company based in Eatontown NJ and Monmouth County"

Keywords could be Oil tank, oil tank removal Eatontown, oil tank removal company Monmouth County. Then the content on the page could be describing how we are top rated, awards the company won etc.

You get the idea. Take a look at a few of your pages so you can begin to see if the SEO on your site is set up to help your website. This information will help you to have a discussion with your agency partner on how to grow your area of opportunities by creating new pages with different keyword focuses.

Note: Search engine optimization takes time. It is not a flip of the switch where you instantly show up for keywords that will drive traffic to your sites just because you updated metadata.

Paid Advertising Strategies

Paid Search/Text Ads

These are the text ads at the top of the page.

A good rule of thumb is to Google your keywords every few days to see if your competition is showing up or bidding on your name with paid ads, which we will discuss in the following section. Remember to have your agency partner provide progress reports each month showing the work they did to your website and any changes in traffic, engagement and conversions.

In most cases, you are paying an agency or someone trained to do these ads. I don't recommend doing paid search ads yourself without the correct training because it can get very expensive very quickly if the campaigns are not set up correctly.

So, Glenn, if I am working on my content to help me come up in organic search, why should I pay for ads?

Good question. The reason you would be paying for this type of advertising is to show up for keywords you are not relevant for right now. Let's say "Carpet Cleaner NJ" is the keyword you want to show up for. When you do the search, you find that your website is on page 2 right now or low on page 1.

Make sure you are having these discussions with your agency partner because this can be a very expensive way to market if someone who is not skilled is running this. You should talk to your agency who can do research to see what the cost would be for clicks on certain keywords.

Let's say we are bidding on "Oil tank removal NJ" and we find it costs $5 per click. You then would discuss/decide how important it is to be in spot one or two and then what should you begin to spend. This is where a trusted agency would come in.

Let's say you decide on a budget of $1000 to be spent over a month. The agency will then decide how to spend a $1000 budget through daily budgets, bidding strategies, daily adjustments, reporting etc.

As you can see, this is not something the untrained should handle.

In the short-term, to make sure you are seen for this keyword, you can create an ad and then set a budget to bid on that keyword. Where you show up in terms of placement will depend on your budget for the month as well as how much you are willing to bid. It's a dual strategy to make sure you are showing up for keywords in your strategy either in organic or paid. Make sure you are having these discussions with your agency partner.

One of the biggest mistakes in these types of campaigns is where the customer is sent once they click. The best user experience is once the customer engages with your ads, they are taken to the specific page on your site that contain the information you spoke about in your ad. If you and your marketing partner do not think this through, you could be wasting your customer's time taking them to a page that has nothing to do with the ad or just to the home page.

What if you gave a customer the wrong physical address to your store, how long do you think they will drive around until they find it? Not long I am sure. The same thing applies to click ads. We want the customer journey to be easy and seamless.

Again, this type of advertising is not for the untrained. You need to partner with someone who is fully versed in understanding budgets both daily and monthly, how to spread your money out across the timeframe for the ad, the best times to display the ads, etc. You and your vendor partner have to be monitoring the analytics and reporting of each campaign, or else you can run through your money very quickly.

Remarketing/Display

Remarketing is a strategy to target those people who have come to your website with your ads. I am sure you have seen these ads on certain websites as you search online. These are the ads that you see that are using the Google display network or Bing network.

How it works: The consumer comes to your website, and a code or cookie is placed in their browser, so when they arrive at sites using the display network, an ad that you have attached to the code is now shown. This gives you an opportunity to follow these customers around for a certain period of time (I recommend thirty days), and then you can replace the ad. If they shut down their computer or clear their cache, the code will go away, but many people never turn off their computer, so this is a very cost-effective way to get your branding message out there.

So think of ads you see. I went to a website for a vendor Curaytor, and later in the day, I was catching up on news at CNN.com. As you can see from this screenshot, their ad is to the right of the news article. Also at the top, notice an ad for an IBM whose site I also visited earlier in the day.

Are you ignorant about the world?

By Hans Rosling and Anders Bolling
🕐 Updated 11:58 AM ET, Sat March 7, 2015

Rosling on a global population shift 01:31

Story highlights

Hans Rosling: Media is built on conflict and a black-and-white model of explanation

The reality of the world is different, and often

Editor's Note: Hans Rosling is co-founder of the Gapminder Foundation in Stockholm. Anders Bolling is a journalist. The views expressed are their own. For more, watch Rosling on Fareed Zakaria GPS this Sunday at 10 a.m. and 1 p.m. ET on CNN.

(CNN) — The world is spinning so fast that it can be hard to

Notice both the ads focus on a short message. More of a branding message than an offer. Think of your message following the visitors to your website around as they move through the Internet.

Remember all advertising requires testing and analysis. Make sure to partner with a company that will explain what they are doing each month, testing different ads to get the most engagement for your marketing dollars. Remember that this strategy also requires a budget, bidding, etc., and a well-thought-out path for the customer to follow.

Now in this case, you may want to create specific landing pages for each campaign or use specific phone tracking numbers so you can associate a number of calls to a project. If the only way someone called a specific number was by seeing your ad or going to a specific landing page, then it is easier to maximize and refine your marketing programs. Without this type of analysis, you will be wasting large amounts of money.

An example of what I mean by testing is often called A/B testing. For instance, in an automotive ad campaign: Is it better to quote the lease price ($299 per month) or interest rate (0% interest for 12 months) or cash back ($1,500 back at signing)? All of these options need to be tested. You will need to keep one ad as your control subject. Remember to only change one thing at a time.

Example: Let's say you currently have a photo of a red car with a message saying

"$299 per month lease." If you are going to test the messages, make sure the rest of the ad remains the same from color of the car, car type, location of car in photo, where the form is on the page. Change the message and then monitor results. If it improves, then make the change to the new ad. Later, you can test other things if you want, but remember to always have a control ad and change only one thing at a time.

Every page on your website can also be tested as well. Does having a person in the ad get more engagement than just showing the product? Should the form be placed at the top or bottom of the page? To the right or left? There are many technologies that can help you see where people are clicking. Crazy Egg is a very popular company. (crazyegg.com)

Everything you are testing should be done to tweak the ads to gain the most conversions or performance you desire from the ad or page (Call, click, form, etc.)

Video Preroll

Preroll is really starting to surge as an advertising form. You may have run across it as you have surfed the web yourself. These are the fifteen to thirty second ads that play (and you try to skip) before you can watch the video you selected. Video preroll has created a love-hate relationship with some viewers.

I spoke to a gentleman whom I was helping with their marketing, and when I mentioned preroll, he said, "I hate those ads." After I explained how effective these ads were as well as cost effective, he then said, "I may grow to love those ads as a marketer."

When you are creating these short videos, you may want to use a commercial that you have already created. That is fine, but remember, it has to be short, to the point with a strong call to action. The call to action should be in the first 5-7 seconds before someone can click past the ad.

I tend to like the ones that have something to engage the consumer.

"Learn the five reasons your carpet is making you sick." "Learn how to get more cash for your trade in."

Another word of caution: These ads must match your "why buy from me" message. They can't be shock value for the sake of clicks. You can't say "save $1,000 right now" only to have them jump through twenty hoops and never really qualify. People don't like bait and switch.

Social Media

I will apologize right now that I will not be going into depth on how to use Social Media to market your business. The reason is, that this topic really deserves a book in and of itself. Social Media advertising is changing so rapidly that anything I say now may be out of date by the time this hits the stores. I will leave this topic for another time. In the mean time I would like to share some great books already written on the subject. Gary Vaynerchuk's "Jab Jab Right Hook" and Guy Kawasaki's "The Art of Social Media" are two I would recommend.

I will leave you with this. Social Media is not going away. Each day new platforms are coming around that people are engaging with. Just because you may not use Social Media or all of the platforms does not mean your business should not engage. My advice is to become a student of social media and how to leverage it in order to get your information in front of consumers online. It is another avenue for your to provide great content that supports your why buy from me message.

Reputation Marketing: Where Yesterday Meets Today

My grandfather started a local music store in the 1950s. He relied on his customers spreading the word that his store was the place you needed to go for musical equipment and lessons. He understood that you needed people to share your message, not just advertising it in the newspaper. Many businesses of that era focused mainly on the local market. You hoped that your advertising reached beyond the city limits but really depended on people to call or walk in from word of mouth.

You advertised (maybe prior to cable TV) in newspapers, in the church bulletin, maybe on the placemats in diners, billboards, supported a local team, etc. You sent cards via mail to consumers or referral marketing by handing business cards out to everyone you met. In my youth, there were even door-to-door salespeople like Amway, and they built their business on your recommendations.

Today the consumer is the one reaching out to the businesses based on their marketing, especially online. One of the main things that is needed today to validate your marketing claims is testimonials or reviews from your previous customers.

I promised you that I would not bore you with statistics, but these are important to see how customers rely on reviews to sort through the information online. These statistics come from the Brightlocal.com Consumer Review Study.

1. Overall use of reviews.

Thirty Five percent of consumers use reviews on a regular basis. Nine out of ten have used reviews regularly or occasionally. I would suspect that based on the price of your product or service increases or they are purchasing your product every few years, reviews become more important.

2. Do you trust reviews as much as personal recommendation?

Eighty percent (80%) say that they trust reviews if they think they are authentic. This statistic shows us that people are now trusting reviews, even from strangers. Reviews are more prevalent, and certain review sites carry more weight, depending on the product or service.

3. How many reviews do you read before trusting a business?

This statistic is telling since people are trusting reviews more.

40% say it takes 1-3 reviews to build trust. 70% say 1-6 reviews are needed. This has increased because more reviews are available so this allows customer to read as many as are needed for them to make a decision.

4. When judging a business what do you look for in regards to reviews?

The top two answers were Star Rating and amount of reviews. That makes sense but the biggest thing I took away was that 70% of consumers needed to see at least 3 stars but 40% needed to have 4 stars or more to even consider a business.

The other big influencer was how recent the reviews were. 70% said that the review needed to be within 2-3 months but over 40% said it had to be within a month.

What these statistics should tell you is that reviews are important to your success online. If consumers now have more information than ever, personal validation of your product or service is needed to cut through the marketing noise. Having a process to encourage a consistent stream of reviews from your customers is no longer optional for the success of your business.

Take a quick test. Google your business name with the word "reviews" after it and see what comes up on the first two pages of search. I said the first two pages because the listings on page 2 can always creep up on to page 1. Take a look at all of the places you may have reviews that you did not know existed.

Now you need to create a strategy to go into each of these listings to see if all of your information is correct, if you can add photos or videos. Remember these are listings people may find, so you need to make sure you control them. Now some of these may have a slight cost attached to them to claim them. You need to decide if they are relevant to your strategy. If they are on page 1, they should be.

Getting Reviews

Do you have a set process in place to ask for reviews? If not, you need to.

I recommend that if you are a brick-and-mortar location, then think of a spot in your sales process, possibly after purchase where you can ask for a review. Maybe there is a small card holder with a flyer asking to have customers tell you how you are doing. The point is you have to have your team asking for reviews as if it matters. I have been to some big box retailers, and as the cashier hands you the receipt, they run through a script, asking for a review with absolutely no enthusiasm. If you do not think my feedback is important, then why should I?

A word of caution: Do not be afraid of a bad review. Your initial reaction may be, "Glenn, but why would I want people to see someone who was not happy?" My response to that is to think of how you shop. What is your reaction to one hundred perfect reviews? Does that make you pause? Everyone knows someone who is never happy no matter what the experience they had was. So then how can every one of your customers be happy? Do you see how that may drive people away instead of bring them in?

It has been said that if you have a negative review it increases the relevance of all your reviews by seven times. Now I am not sure if that is true, but I personally feel it gives you a truer presence in the mind of your potential customers. What is more important is how you respond to your reviews, both positive and negative. My recommendation is to respond to every negative review and around 50 to 60% of the positive reviews.

If you don't pay attention to your business reviews then any negative review stands out there as potentially true. I recommend responding to them very simply:

"I am sorry we did not meet your standards. Our goal is to exceed customer expectations. I would love to discuss this with you offline. Please call my direct number or e-mail me here. Glenn Pasch owner or whatever title."

Make sure that it is a direct email and phone number versus a generic customer service e-mail or phone number. You want to stand behind your service to deliver the personal experience you have marketed to them initially.

By responding to reviews, this will show future customers that you care about your customers and gives potential customers the feeling that if they ever have a problem, someone will be there to help. This is still very important to people, even in the digital age.

Never get into an argument online even if you know you are right. You will always be seen as a bully. I always like to compare online to real life. Think of yourself in a restaurant and you overhear a customer say the service was not great and the manager began to argue and tell the customer they are wrong.

"You would not know good food." "You do not know good food." "Our service is great." "Why don't you leave." "We do not need your money, etc."

I know this may be a little extreme, but would you come back? Or would you be afraid to come back. God forbid if you had a complaint.

Video Testimonials:

If you can convince one of your customers to send in their own video, with their comments and feedback instead of you asking the questions it will be even more effective.

Keep it short asking only 4-5 questions about their experience:

- What was the reason they came in?
- Did we meet expectations?
- Who did they deal with?
- Are they local or did they drive from a different city? (You can use this video to help target other cities)
- Would they recommend your business to others?

Once you have the video, as we discussed previously, you need to optimize it correctly and use it on your website, in content or in social media.

One tip for using video testimonials on a website: make them easy to find. Maybe have a button or icon on the home page directing visitors to these videos. Also make sure that the videos match your customer base. Individuals like to click on videos that look like themselves. One word of warning. If the video is going to play automatically, make sure there is a mute button or pause button easily accessible. Think if someone is at work when visiting your website, what would happen if the video started playing at a high volume, the consumer may just hit the back button and not return to your site.

One question I am asked is how many videos do you need? I would say that you should get one new video every month. This would be a great place to begin. Remember the statistic on reviews being recent. We need to see current customers being happy with your service.

Having a solid strategy to garner reviews will help you to validate your marketing and increase customer interest.

Mobile

As we discuss the growth of mobile and what that means to your marketing, there is currently a big discussion of having an adaptive or responsive website. At the time of writing this book, Google has announced it will penalize websites that are not mobile friendly. This shows us once again that a search engines' focus is providing a great user experience for their customers, and we have to adapt.

One other thing to be aware of is the growth of the use of multiple devices during the shopping process. Make sure that potential customers can easily view your marketing on a mobile device.

Think of your own behavior or your children's where you are watching TV with your tablet or phone nearby. Maybe checking social media or tweeting out something about what you are seeing or checking online about a company whose commercial you saw on TV.

What do consumers find when they search for you or your business on these devices? Here is our website on a tablet:

STAY IN TOUCH

But only if you want the latest news in digital marketing

SIGN UP FOR OUR NEWSLETTER

Real People. Real Strategies. Real Results.

Basically, we're a team of individuals working towards one common goal: providing our clients with a customized, personal, and unparalleled digital experience. Our NJ digital marketing company is composed of real people from all walks of life collaborating and innovating daily to be the best in the internet marketing business—and that's exactly what we are.

Social Media Branding

People are talking online.
Let's get them talking about you.

Paid Search

Look what your target market just found—
Your PPC and SEM that works.

Remarketing

That potential customer that got away?
We can get them back for you.

WHAT'S NEW

Here is our site on a smartphone. I will put three photos so you can see what you can access as you scroll down. Notice again easy to find "our services."

But what if I just did a search on my mobile phone for PCG?

PCG Digital Marketing Agency | NJ Internet ...
www.pcgdigitalmarketing.com

Mobile-friendly - An NJ-based **digital** marketing agency that specializes in SEO, content creation, social media advertising, paid search, ...

NJ Digital Marketing Careers | Join PCG Digital Marketing
www.pcgdigitalmarketing.com › careers

Mobile-friendly - If you are in search of a challenging job in the SEO, SEM, and broader internet marketing field, check out the open ...

Meet Our Team - PCG Digital Marketing
www.pcgdigitalmarketing.com › meet-ou...

Mobile-friendly - Meet the characters that make our NJ **digital** marketing company the best place to be. Our diverse team is ready to get ...

PCG Digital Marketing Reviews | Glassdoor

My point is that on a mobile phone, having a good paid search strategy can show up in search and make the experience easy for customers to find you. By the way, pay attention to see if your competition is bidding on your name for paid advertising.

Vendor Partners

This is a topic I do not mince words with. There are a lot of charlatans in the online marketing field taking advantage of business owners who do not understand the terminology. I have seen reports designed to hide poor performance by focusing on a metric that is doing well, whether that metric is impactful or not.

Just because you can spout the terms of digital marketing or knowing what SEO is does not make you a good marketer. Just because you know how to market in the traditional area but you hired some hot young kid who can code a website does not make you a digital agency.

This section is very important in helping you find the right vendor partner. Make sure that your vendor is willing to take the time to explain everything they are doing in a language you can understand. If you do not understand something, make sure to ask questions. Do not hesitate because you may feel uneducated on the subject. You are paying the vendor a fee and deserve to understand what they are doing each month for their fee. You deserve vendor transparency.

If the vendor is unwilling to explain their process or tasks they executed or just continue to send a long list of "things we do each month," then it is time to change vendors.

Understand that some digital marketing takes time to show results, but the vendor should be setting the right expectations out of the gate so you are not looking for results too soon.

Here is what I recommend to all of my potential customers or to attendees of my workshops.

- Get references.
  - o Ask for ten to twenty. Don't let the agency or vendor get by with giving you their prized two clients who love them. Get a variety of clients from different industries, sizes of business, and also length of time they have been clients. It would be interesting to speak to long-term clients to see how the relationship evolved and also how the vendor continues to provide value.
  - o Ask for the names of two clients who recently terminated their services. It would be interesting to hear what factors made them move on to another agency. Price? Service levels? Hired staff internally? This should not be overlooked as a way to decide on a vendor partner.

- Ask How the Vendor Trains their staff
  - o Are they Google/Bing certified?
  - o Do they do ongoing training?

- Ask how the vendor will communicate progress.
  - o Monthly reporting
  - o Weekly/Monthly calls
  - o Client education versus just sending reports
  - o Ongoing strategy

- Does the vendor participate in the digital marketing industry?
  - o Do they write for industry magazines or blogs?
  - o Do they speak at digital marketing events?
  - o Have they written any books on their specialty skills?

- How is the vendor's digital presence?
  - o Is their website informative and easy to read?
  - o What type of content do you find when you Google their name?
  - o How are their reviews online?
  - o Do they have client testimonials?
  - o Do they use video and social media to promote their business?
  - o How is their mobile website?

Budgeting, Reporting, and Accountability

One question I am asked is how much of the marketing budget should be dedicated to online marketing. Well, that depends. I know that sounds like I am avoiding the subject, but there are many factors that I discuss with business owners.

- Do they have any budget currently dedicated to online marketing?
- If we need to adjust, are we keeping the same overall marketing budget, or are there more funds available?
- What is the business owner's tolerance for new marketing?
- Do they have internal staff who will be doing the creation of content and marketing, or are they also going to have to hire an agency to do the work?

These questions are important because if the ownership has no previous budget, then spending new money can be something they did not plan on. Moreover, having to spend money on something with no frame of reference in terms of what amount should be spent, then what seems normal to the marketer seems outrageous to the owner.

What I am seeing with many of my clients, depending on their market, is anywhere from 40% to 80% of their marketing budget being dedicated to online resources. In very competitive markets, offline marketing may not be generating the results it had in the past, so in a rare case or two, 100% of their budget is dedicated to online marketing. But that is a rare occurrence.

Why so many owners are unsure of what they should be doing is the lack of transparent reporting by vendors today. Too often vendors send long multipage reports to their clients to impress (or swamp) them with a large volume of information versus actionable reports.

Every vendor may have different reports, so to claim one is better than another seems a waste of time. *But*, as I mentioned in the vendor selection section, your vendor should be providing you with reports that you can easily understand and show very clearly what tasks they have completed in the previous month, what results have occurred in the past months, as well as what their strategy will be in the coming months.

Do not be afraid to align yourself with an advisor to help you navigate the vendor community. Your monthly marketing budget is not insignificant, so asking for help will benefit your efficiency in the long run.

The On-Demand Economy

Online marketing is not going away. Leaders need to understand how to maximize their marketing dollars in this new medium. More importantly, they have to understand the metrics they will be reviewing as well as how to manage the marketing roles and responsibilities of others in their company.

I was listening to a podcast recently, and the speaker mentioned the term "On-Demand Society" when discussing this ever-growing desire from consumers—to have things at their fingertips—is changing business as we know it. What struck me is how this desire for on-demand services will affect every business in the future. Businesses cannot sit on the sidelines to see if the On-Demand Economy will succeed or fail before jumping in. I think it is here to stay and will evolve even more.

It is easy to understand the On-Demand Economy when we think of media consumption and the growth of media companies that now have their content on-demand. I see the future of this economy in my young children who are so comfortable accessing their shows or working their online apps across multiple devices. It seems that in the future, they will have no frame of reference to what we are speaking about when we say that one has to wait for something. Slow downloads are painful for them right now. Speed matters.

I bring this up because even a year ago, businesses across the board were not really embracing the On-Demand Economy. The feedback I read was that it works for some industries but "not for mine." With the increase of on-demand services and "content when I want it," websites now have to be informational hubs.

This is why your online marketing and the efficiency of your website must be thought of in terms of the journey you are taking consumers on. From offline to online and then potentially to your doorstep, consumers are looking to control the journey.

One of the biggest failures of marketing is that I see a great promotion or award online and then when I show up at the brick-and-mortar location, it is nowhere to be seen. You have not connected your marketing. This creates doubt in the buyer's mind, and with the ability to share their pleasure or displeasure online, you have to control this journey.

Offline Media by Troy Spring

In this section, my goal is to break down the confusion of offline media as well as show you that this type of advertising is still a valuable way to attract business. I also want to help you to understand what your vendors are saying as they are helping you create your connected marketing mix.

Now before we begin, you may wonder why the authors refer to this type of media as offline marketing versus traditional marketing. In my opinion, the words "traditional media" have almost become negative or old-fashioned in many minds because of the digital explosion we are living through at this moment in time. I could not disagree more.

So for the purposes of this book and the future of great advertising, we will refer to it as offline media / traditional media is alive and well!

Prior to reading this segment of the book, I think it is prudent to mention I am a huge fan of digital (online) media. I agreed to write this book with Glenn Pasch (the primary author of this book) because we do not feel it is a competition between the two media types like many do. The most successful businesses see the connection between both worlds.

My goal is to arm you with facts and education so that if or when someone approaches you to tell you that offline media is over, you can calmly reason with them and discuss the value. I point this out because the viability of offline media is under scrutiny like never before.

In today's market place, many companies have begun to shift the advertising dollars they once only used for offline media (TV, radio, direct mail, newspapers, billboards, etc.) towards online media. My only advice is that when this happens, make sure that you are receiving correct reporting and allow the offline vendor to work with the online media vendor to connect your marketing.

Thus the title of the book, *The Power of Connected Marketing*.

I recall talking to an auto dealer at a conference in Dallas. He mentioned that he switched his marketing efforts to using only online advertising for his dealership in Chicago. I applauded him since I felt that made sense for his market. To run a dominant schedule of offline advertising in Chicago would be very, very expensive and not cost effective for many small- to medium- sized businesses.

The unfortunate part of this example and the reason I felt this book (in particular, this segment) was needed is that many businesses in some small towns all the way up to medium-sized cities are discounting the workhorse-like efforts of offline media.

As you move through this section it will be broken out into two areas of focus.

First, I would like you to see clearly how and why offline media is still, a very viable part, if not the workhorse of marketing efforts for many businesses.

Second, I will do my best to explain how to buy media and to help you define whether or not you, your business, and marketing dollars are right for either a long-term or short- term offline campaigns.

Note: this section may be a little technical but I will do my best to keep it easy to follow.

Okay, let's go!

Why Offline Media is Still Viable

I will focus my comments on regionally targeted advertising. I feel this will be more useful for small to mid-size business owners that make up a majority of the advertisers today.

Allow me to paint the picture of a conversation I may have with a business in regards to their marketing. An owner of a business may say, "We tried radio and TV" or "We do radio and TV now, and it doesn't seem to be working."

My first request would be to have the business owner show me what exactly they are currently doing. Remember we cannot adjust unless we know what is currently happening.

What I often see is that the business did not execute a full on media strategy. They "dabbled" as I like to say. It is very hard to judge the effectiveness of any media campaign, especially offline media, unless you have put yourself in a position to be successful.

In my opinion, as much as 50% of ad dollars spent on offline media, if not up to 70%, are wasted dollars because they did not have the right strategy. This is caused by both the lack of education on the part of the buyer and having the right vendor partner. It is sad to say but you have to remember that sometimes the agency partner's business model is revenue driven. They have media spots or what I call inventory that needs to be sold, and so they work out a cost effective package just to get it sold. It may not garner the right results for the client but the inventory was sold.

Now before you think I am being too hard on vendors (refer to Glenn's section of Finding the Correct Vendor Partner), there are many great agencies and vendors. It is just that those of you who are doing the buying of media need to know the right questions to ask and I hope I am providing them.

The following pages will help you figure out whom to trust and what a good marketing plan looks like so you feel more comfortable with these tough decisions.

Before we can begin to buy any type of media or sit down to have a conversation with a sales rep from an agency or media outlet, you need to understand the following four points. These four items will help you buy all media correctly in the future and be able to adapt and change strategy as needed.

Let's learn about The Four Pillars of Advertising.

The Four Pillars of Advertising

The four pillars of advertising are exactly that: pillars. Do not discount any of the pillars, as they are all important. Without all four pillars being part of an ad campaign, the campaign will surely fail. Notice I did not say more than likely fail. No, I was pretty clear on what word I chose, *will*. It will fall flat on its face and it will hurt your bottom line.

When purchasing any media, including online or offline, you should always look at these pillars. Use them as a guide to help you make a more educated decision. If you notice the absence of one or more, it should throw up a red flag and warn you that you are about to waste money.

The four major pillars to take into consideration when buying offline media are:

1. Reach
2. Frequency
3. Creative
4. Cost

Before I dive deep into each, let me break down each of these words for you.

Reach: How many people will hear/see your message. Think of Audience size.

Frequency: How often your ad will be heard/seen by a listener or viewer.

Creative: The actual ad/message/commercial

Cost: What the cost is for the media buy. We will discuss different metrics later.

So in a simple statement: When you **reach** enough people with a strong **creative** message and those people hear it so many times (**frequency**), it has become second nature to them. Your core message has been branded into their brains. You will have moved a market. The only pillar in question is **cost**. So if you can do all three at a **cost** that allows you to make a suitable ROI, all ads are worth it.

Ok. Let's pause because I said we will be heading into some technical things but if you understand these four pillars and how each of them support the other, then we can begin to build up your knowledge of buying media.

Great. Let's move on.

Let's look at an example: Some people think that the newspaper is a dying medium. What if you could buy the entire back page **(creative)** for $1 **(cost)** every Sunday for the next 10 weeks **(frequency)** when the circulation (**reach**) is its highest. Would you do it even if people told you newspapers are dying?

I would think so because you looked at all four pillars and felt that it is going to *reach* enough people, I can put a strong *creative* message on it, and the *cost* is right. As a matter of fact, the cost was so good that you did it without even taking *frequency* into consideration.

Are you beginning to see how the four pillars all need to be addressed? If you changed any of those pillars, maybe the cost was $100 or $500, or maybe it was half a page or was not the back page, or maybe it was only a one time ad, all of those changes would affect your decision.

We are going to dive a little deeper into each pillar to help you really understand how they all really work. Before we begin, I am going to need to give you a small glossary of terms that will help you understand the next section.

Glossary of Terms for Offline Media Buying:

Flight of Media: This is the total media spend and schedule of the ads.

Share of the Market: share is the percent of the total of the market segment being reached. Particularly in electronic media, each station has a % of the total viewers or listeners.

<u>Market Segment:</u> a piece of the total population. Example a segment could be listeners or viewers between the ages of 25-35.

<u>GRPs:(gross rating points)-</u> this is when you multiply reach by frequency. This metric is used to measure to overall effectiveness in your marketing efforts. We also sometimes refer to them as "grips". IE: How much is your grip getting?

Reach: The goal of creating reach with your ads is trying to figure out which stations you play your ad on. There is never really just one station that has everyone in the market. Think of your own viewing or listening habits. There are hundreds of TV channels and hundreds of radio stations.

So you will need to build a flight (your media schedule) with multiple stations and/or channels to achieve our goal of reach. Our goal should be to try and reach 60 to 70% plus of the market.

You figure this out by adding up the share of the market each station has. Remember that the share is the percent of the total of that market segment being reached by that station.

Example of market share:

In your market the number of Adult listeners 25 to 54 is 100,000. Radio station WXX has a 6.5 share of the market.

Though not completely accurate, you can imagine approximately 6,500 people from that segment are listening to that station.

If you only advertise on their station, even if frequency is high, the reach is not enough to have an impact.

Let's now look at an example of how you can use multiple stations to reach more of the market and truly impact your business.

- Station number 1 has an eleven share.
- Station number 2 has a seven share.
- Station number 3 has an eighteen share.
- Station number 4 has a ten share.
- Station number 5 has a nine share.

If we add up all of the stations together we get a total reach of 55% of the market. This means that 55% of the markets total population within the segment of adults will hear your ad. In this example, you can imagine fifty-five thousand people.

Much more reach than using one station.

Before we move into discussing frequency, we need to take a moment discuss the metric called GRP: (Gross Rating Points). This was not listed as one of the four pillars but it is important to understand.

The easiest way to think about GRP is this: When you multiply the reach by the frequency, you get the GRPs (gross rating points). It is a quick number to manage if you will get your message to your audience in an optimal way. What I believe is the optimal GRP is four hundred GRPs weekly. This is my recommended target to make a significant effort at moving a market to action.

Let me give you an example because I do not want to lose you in technical terms.

In our example above, our station mix has a reach of 55%. In order to hit my 400 GRP I would need to have a frequency of 8. (400/55) In simple terms it means that 55% of the market heard the spot 8 times each in a period of just one week. I call this hardwiring because it takes multiple times for a listener to remember your ad.

Let's say that using our station mix of 55% market share, the agency recommends a GRP of 250 because of cost. Well now you can divide the 250 (GRP) by 55 (reach) and see that your frequency will only be 4.5 times. Now you then have to decide if hearing your ad 4 times or 8 times is better for your business.

I am doing my best to keep it simple and I hope you see how to break down this marketing into simple terms. How many people can hear my ad and how often do they.

It can be easy to cut your schedule down and take away stations or even spots and frequency each week and think it won't hurt much. But it does. It can be devastating to cut even fifty GRP. It can be very easy to do if your decision makers are more budget-driven than formula-driven. Swallowing the cost of running the right formula can be daunting.

Let's look at it a different way. Think of boiling water. At 200 degrees, water is just hot water. I am sure somewhere in time, someone tried to cook rice or pasta in hot water. It may have been palatable, but it was never right. But at 212 degrees, the magic of boiling happened.

The same can be said for 400 GRP. If you tamper with 400 GRPs, you can have some palatable results but never just right. But once you hit 400 GRPs, it is like boiling the water. So my warning is that I would not tamper with that formula much, or you could end up with wet soggy and unappealing results like poorly cooked rice.

So let's move to frequency and put it all together.

Frequency: The goal of frequency is finding the right amount of times the ad is heard in order to hardwire it into our heads. I am sure there are ads we hear all the time and can't get out of our heads. They had the right frequency.

So I am asked if there is a right number and I believe that a frequency of six or seven times a week would be perfect, especially if you want to move the market fast.

Note: I like to break these metrics down into weeks, not months. Some reps will give you a monthly frequency number, and sometimes if you are buying a multiple-month TV schedule, you may get a total frequency number. I cannot blame the reps for doing this.

I mean telling a client they have a twelve frequency over three months sounds better than a one frequency over a week. So just remember to always divide your total frequency into weekly times and strive for six to seven. Remember to look at total mix because even a 5 frequency with a large share can be useful to the mix.

So let's review our previous example and add in frequency.

- Station 1 has an eleven share/ Frequency 7
- Station 2 has a seven share/Frequency 7
- Station 3 has an eighteen share/Frequency 8
- Station 4 has a ten share/Frequency 5
- Station 5 has a nine share/Frequency 9

Let's now make sure our mix has the right GRP

- Station 1: 11 x 7= 77 GRP
- Station 2: 7 x 7 = 49 GRP
- Station 3: 18 x 8 = 144 GRP
- Station 4: 10 x 5 = 50 GRP
- Station 5: 9 x 9 = 81 GRP

Total GRP = 401

Be very, very careful not to spread your marketing frequency out over a longer period of time. Some small businesses may be tempted to take the cost of this media buy and split it up over two weeks or even four. This will diminish your GRPs to 200 or even 100 per week.

Remember what I said about your rice cooking in 212 degree boiling water. Would you prefer 4 weeks of raw rice that never cooked or one good meal of perfectly cooked rice or spaghetti? Our suggestion is always that if you can only afford one week of a 400 GRP schedule, then only do one week of it. This is especially true for an event-style transactional selling when you need to move product on a given weekend!

I know you may be thinking, "Troy, why is this so important?"

I cannot stress this enough that if your goal is to hardwire your message into the consumer's brain you cannot water it down because it will lose its impact.

Think of the four pillars. If you have good reach, a good creative but cost affects frequency, well then your building is leaning and in danger of falling over.

Let's move on to the next pillar: Creative

Creative: This pillar to me is where many small companies who are doing their creative work without the proper education will falter. Even some of the biggest agencies in the world get lost when it comes to creative.

What do I mean by agencies getting lost when it comes to creative? Some agencies rely simply on the numbers to decide how to buy media. They may understand reach and frequency very well but not how important creative is. After all, numbers do not lie. Well, in this case, they can.

If you have terrific reach and frequency but the creative is "so what," you could waste lots and lots and lots of money. After all, four hundred GRPs a week does not come cheap.

Remember the four pillars. Even if the buy of the media is brilliant, if the creative is poor, it is still a total waste of money. I hope you are seeing why I am constantly referring to the four pillars. They are all connected.

Let's look at this in another light. Many of us have heard that a terrific stereo system is only as good as its speakers. The circuitry of the stereo could be the best in the world but if the speakers are bad you will never ever hear how great the stereo or music really is.

Let's now apply this to an example of a business buying poor media. If they buy a poor media flight of reach and frequency (speakers) and then put a bad creative (song) on it to boot . . . don't blame the station (Stereo) or the radio or TV for you not getting the sound you wanted out of your system.

It takes all three for you to really love the music it can make.

So now imagine in this example the creative is great. If you do not have the right speaker (reach/frequency) it still does not connect.

However, play the right memorable message (creative) through with a well-planned and well-executed media buy with the right reach and frequency to hardwire that memorable and hard-driving message into the consumer's ears and brain, and you will find that you like the sound of that music.

I wrote a lot about creative here because it is the intangible. You cannot get a report that tells you how good it is. You have to have an ear or eye for it. It is a talent that not many people in the world really get right, and without getting it right, all the other parts fall apart. The message here is to take your creative very seriously.

Now let me take a moment to discuss intentionally bad creative. Ever see a really bad commercial and say, "Wow, that was horrible"? Sometimes this is a planned strategy to get you or the audience talking about the ad. At the end of the day, your goal is to be remembered. Any extra exposure can help maximize the marketing spend for the right company at the right time.

Note: In closing on this section of the creative, in my opinion the worst creative is the one that falls into the category of "*so what.*" Do not settle on creative that does not cause a reaction. This pillar can easily topple the whole campaign.

Cost: Cost is always a fun discussion. It has so many sides to it, starting with the fact there can be a hesitation to spend money, and most people are rightfully afraid of wasting it.

I am aware that you can run your business into the ground if you spend foolishly. Yes, I understand that marketing has to be affordable for your company. Any vendor you work with should have the approach of: "We don't want a client to spend too much, and we do not want them to spend too little. We want them to spend *the right amount*."

So what is the right amount? That really does depend on the goals of the advertiser, but for me the right amount is the amount that it takes you to run the formula. In some markets, that could be very low and in others, it can give a business owner a heart attack. The difference you ask? It is simply the population that hears your ad most of the time.

Before we continue we need to introduce another cost tracking metric that is used to decide where to place your ads based on cost to reach 1000 listeners.

CPM: Cost to Reach 1000 listeners
(Troy Tip: "M" is the Roman numeral for 1000)

CPM is calculated by multiplying reach and frequency and then dividing by 1000 and then dividing the cost to run the ad by this result. (I know, I know. Pretty confusing to keep track of so let's go to the example!!!)

Example: 100,000 people in market and two different stations to choose from.

Station number 1 has an 11 share and a 5.5 frequency and the cost to run the ad at that station is $1,400 a week.

100,000 people in market with an 11 share is 11,000 people who hear the spot 5.5 times in a week, which would be 55,000 times the ad is heard. Divide that by 1,000 listeners and you have 55. (Meaning there is 55 groups of 1000 listeners.)

$1,400 divided by 55 = $25.00 CPM

Station number 2 has and 18 share and a 7 frequency, and the cost to run the ad at this station is $2,500 a week.

100,000 people in the market with an 18 share is 18,000 people who hear the ad 7 times in a week, which would be 126,000 times the ad is heard. Divide that by 1,000 listeners and you end up with 126.

$2,500 divided by 126 = $19 CPM

The mistake that some businesses will make, that do not understand this formula, is to pick the station that costs only $1,400 a week. They may also tell the second station that they have to come down to $1400 number if they want their business.

But now that you understand this formula, you can see that in reality it would be smarter to tell station 1 that they need to come down to the CPM of station 2, which is only $19 per thousand reached versus $25. The station that cost $2,500 per week here was a much better value. This example shows you how easy it can be to make an uneducated mistake and fail to spend wisely.

My goal is to arm you with the right formulas and facts to determine the best value. It takes the guesswork and emotion out of your marketing discussion and helps you to feel more in control and spend your dollars far more wisely.

Note: A good goal to shoot for is to see if you can get your CPMs to $10.00 for radio. That is only a benchmark I try to shoot for with my clients. We pay less in some areas, and we pay more in others, especially for a top-ranked station. It is a good guide. For TV, we use $18. Again, just a guide-less in some cases, more in others.

Remember this does not account for your total budget, newspaper, direct mail, etc. These are just a few guides for you to use for TV and radio spend.

I have run across industries where manufacturers or associations share certain benchmark metrics for their members to use and follow. I will submit that they have a very good system and their intention is to help keep their members in line with spending, etc., to maintain profitability.

That said, now that you understand the formula, you can feel more empowered to decide if you want to just follow the pack or decide for yourself what is the right amount for your business.

Just as I have seen people disregard this number and spend much more only to be wildly successful, I have seen business owners suffer because they try so hard to work within those guides.

Remember, it is your business; and if you are in a very average town with the perfect middle ground product and in business for the perfect amount of time, you may very well be able to use the guide and be very successful.

However, it is more than likely that your business is not perfectly average. Let's say you are in a smaller town outside a larger area, and you need to get people to drive to your business.

That makes you a destination business so it makes sense that you would need to spend more than the average to get the business to your door, right?

So here is your choice. Follow the guide, spend the average amount but because you didn't advertise enough, the people did not hear your message enough and did not see any value in making that drive to leave their hometown.

The good news in following the guidelines is your average advertising cost is going to look really good on your financial statement. The bad news is that your net profits are going to be horrible. It is really not a good choice.

However, if you are willing to work the formula, spend a little more aggressively so customers hear your message, then they can see the value of driving out to visit your business and then you can compete and win.

I know your advertising line will look higher, which some may think is bad news, but your net profits will be higher which is really the number to judge your results.

In closing, *Cost* as a pillar is simply this.

Find a cost so that you can afford the right formula and a media buy that makes sense to your business. I would rather you do it correctly for a shorter period of time than to try and spread it out and weaken the impact.

If you hit the medias hard one week a month, People will eventually say… "They always have something going on there." Even more than you would with a watered down approach all month long. Simply put when you Hit them, Hit them hard. They will feel it and remember it.

Now that we have discussed all of the four pillars, I hope that you see how they are all connected. The formulas may have been a little technical but my goal in sharing them is to provide a resource in this book that you can use as a tool to aid in your future decisions.

The Different Media and What Makes Them Work or Not Work

Now that you have the basic fundamentals of buying electronic media (TV and radio), we are going to dive into some good and bad creative for all types of media. For each one of them, I will do my best at explaining what is good and what is bad about them from a creative standpoint.

Understanding that all creative is art and art can be interpreted many different ways I will try and highlight extreme highs and lows in my examples. This way, interpretation won't play so much of a part in seeing good vs. bad.

Beyond that, I will share in this section, I will share some of the advantages or disadvantages each media has.

Note: Remember, as you read this section, that creative is a pillar. Poor creative can make a campaign crumble and fall no matter how good reach, frequency, and cost are.

Billboards

I want to start with billboards because it is easy to see the difference between a good example and a bad one.

Here are some very simple rules when it comes to billboard creative.

Rule 1: Make sure that you use seven words or less. More than seven words takes too long to read for a person driving by. It also makes the words too small to read.

This rule is really important especially when you are working with smaller signs that are called poster boards. Poster boards are normally ten- to twenty-four-feet billboards that you see on the side of the road, normally not as high in the air as a larger forty-eight-foot billboards you may find on a highway.

Rule 2: Pictures are worth a thousand words. They can evoke many emotions and if done right, these types of billboards can be very effective for many businesses.

Here is an example of exemplary billboard creative:

Photo, concept, design & posting courtesy
of Adams Outdoor Advertising.

The use of the "tightrope walker" is brilliant. This is why this board made it into the book. Let me share the story of how I came to find this billboard. One of our staff and a really smart guy called me one morning driving to the office. He was telling me he just saw the craziest thing. He was looking at a restaurant billboard (which was the side he saw coming from the opposite direction) and said there was a guy on top of the billboard tightrope walking. He continued and explained it was cold and windy out, and this guy must be crazy.

I called a friend of mine that works for the local billboard company and asked about this crazy story. He laughed and stated, "It was for a dealership client, and your employee was seeing the wrong side." More importantly, he went on to say that this billboard has been a popular topic of discussion in the local area.

That is the beauty of the tightrope walker extension. (an extension, in billboard terms, is anything that reaches outside the normal edges of a billboard and is an add-on. Here, the tightrope walker is the extension).

I believe Jonah Berger, the author of one of my favorite marketing books, would have called it contagious. In his book *Contagious* Mr. Berger focuses on why some products and marketing catches on and others do not. I recommend reading this book. Back to our billboard, it accomplished its goal and caught on in the public's mind!

Next notice how this billboard follows Rule 1 by using only six words to grab attention. "Crazy. Even Crazier Deals, This Exit." Simple and gets their point across. Want an "CRAZY DEAL"? Turn here and stop at our dealership. The use of the extensions and arrows says it all. I particularly like how they use the arrow to point to the "crazy" guy tightrope walking and the other arrow to point the even more crazy deals, Next Exit. This is an example of terrific creative advertising!

I am asked if logos count towards the 7-word count in Rule 1. Great question. In this case the six words are the ones you count toward the seven you should use. In this case the logo is easy to read so I would not stress about it. In many cases logos or some brand names are instantly recognizable that do not need time to process what they mean.

As a consumer driving by this billboard, you look up, you see the guy walking the tightrope, and read the caption. You laugh. You tell people about it, and they say, "What dealership is that for?" You then say the magic words that the advertiser and the business wanted you to. "Lehigh Valley Honda Acura Hyundai."

The fact that you remembered this message was uniquely positive because most creative on billboards is not even worth looking at. Many times the colors are bad, the words are not written well and they often break Rule 1 by having too many words. I would say that billboard advertising is the easiest of advertising to end up in the land of "so what" when done poorly.

The reason it is so easy to squarely fall in the land of "so what" is that there is no sound, no movement to catch a consumer's eyes, and you only have six seconds maximum before the viewer drives by. These are not problems that radio and TV face. Not to mention that a consumer is supposed to be paying attention to the road during those six seconds.

Poor use of billboard space

Here is an example, in my opinion, of poor billboard advertising. Without getting too far ahead of ourselves, let's just refer to our two rules.

Rule 1: Use Less that 7 words. As you can see they far exceed it with 30 words, not counting their contact information. Remember I mentioned that when you have to many words they become too small to read in 6 seconds. Try it now. Turn you head away and then look back; move the book side to side and in 6 seconds tell me what the sign said. Not easy.

Rule 2: Pictures can have a big impact. They evoke emotions. Ok, what emotions does this photo evoke? It looks like one person is happy and another is not. Even if you had time to really look at this, why is one realtor frowning. Would you want them helping you?

Another great billboard:

Now let's look at one more billboard that does a great job at following both rules.

First they use extensions really well to catch your attention. What caught my eye first was why the corner is folded and over her mouth. This is a brilliant use of the space.

Notice between the picture the ingenious way they used the board and the fold (like the tightrope extension) and just 5 words. This was a home run in my opinion. Great marketing equals brand recognition and sales.

If you are going to use billboards, as you can see following these two rules can help you review creative to make sure it has an impact.

So what are some of the advantages and disadvantages of billboards?

Disadvantages: I would have to say that it could get expensive quickly. In order to really pull off a campaign that will drive traffic to your business with measurable results, you may have to buy multiple billboards.

Sometimes three or four may do it if strategically placed on roads that are going in and out of your town and will be seen by a high percentage of the population in your town or target market area. I have seen campaigns use as many as thirty to forty boards to accomplish their goal. It will definitely put you in a dominant position towards success, assuming the creative is correct but it is a lot more expensive to do this.

Though I am discussing a possible disadvantage here with multiple billboards and potential high cost, it is worth noting the advantage of this as well.

Billboards, in particular, "static"(Not digital) billboards, differ from electronic media because once the digital spot is off the air, it is gone, poof . . . history. Unless you bought the correct frequency your potential customer will never hear it again.

If your billboard is placed in the right spot with high reach (with billboards, they call it D>E>C or daily effective circulation), you will more than likely reap rewards of high frequency when people drive by multiple times in a month. If you are able to get a good cost and put up some strong creative, well, you now have the four pillars.

You may think billboards are old fashioned or not effective but if the reach, the frequency, the cost, and the creative are all right, it can be a winner.

Wouldn't you love to have people driving down that road, saying to one another, "That billboard is coming up" or "Hey, check it out! There is that billboard I was telling you about." You know it happens because I am sure there are few billboards you remember. Think of the two rules and see if that is the reason you remember them. Others have been successful using billboards and now so can you.

<u>Disadvantage:</u> You may have to sign a long contract to get lower rates. In this case it becomes very important for you to get the creative right and be sure that the reach and frequency is good, or your budget can be wasted fast.

<u>Advantage:</u> In small towns, the use of billboards and/or cable should be your focus if you do not have local radio stations. Billboards will reach your local audience without having to spend the dollars it would take on radio, newspaper or network TV in a larger market.

In small markets, I recommend focusing on media that is localized and costs the right amount of money for the amount of people you will want to reach. Buying more expensive media to reach people forty- five minutes away in a larger market that may have no reason to come to your town is not something I recommend.

But think if you could get a few billboards on the busy roads on that 45 minute drive at a more effective cost and I think you can see how billboards might be a great addition to your marketing mix.

Here is a chart that can help you understand how to decide if a billboard is going to have the impact you want. Remember we discussed you judge it by the DEC or Daily Effective

Circulation. How many people will see it going one way in a day? This helps you understand the pillars of reach and frequency. Remember you are handling great creative and cost in different conversations.

Daily Effective Circulation (DEC): The average number of persons potentially exposed to an advertising display.

12 hours (unilluminated - 6:00 am to 6:00 pm) or
18 hours (illuminated - 6:00 am - 12:00 midnight) or
24 hours (illuminated - 6:00 am - 6:00 pm)

DEC Calculator

Enter Official Traffic Count:
(in two directions)

Enter Hours illuminated: 12◯   18◯   24◯

Calculate

Daily Effective Circulation
(in one direction)

 You can Google a Daily Effective Calculator to find something similar.

Advantage: When you are dominant on one of the electronic media like radio or TV, a billboard with a high DEC can be a great way to add more frequency to your campaign. Imagine if someone is driving down the road to work, they hear your radio spot six to seven times a week (our frequency goal) and as they drive home they see your billboard every night with a consistently themed message.

If the radio buy costs $40,000 a month and the billboards to catch them on their drive either in or out of town cost only $5,000, I would call it a great augment to your radio marketing spend to get maximum value for approximately 12% more.

TV

In this section I will talk about the rules that make a good TV spot versus a bad one. I will not refer to specific commercials because not all of you may have seen them. It will be a little harder to visualize because this is not an interactive book. (yet!!)

Rule 1: The first six to eight seconds of the commercial has to be engaging. You have to grab attention immediately. In this day of high definition TV, the quality of colors, fonts and imagery has to be of high quality. You cannot expect to win people over with poor production values. The quality of the production will speak directly to the consumer about the quality of your business.

Rule 2: If you are going to mention reasons to do business with you, make sure your message or claim is unique. I would recommend that you re-read Glenn's section on "Why Buy From Me".

The reason why some TV spots fail at this rule is because their message is uninspiring. Very few people really care that you have been around for seventy-five years. They may care that you offered a discount if it was unique and not just screaming price at them.

Rule 3: No one cares how many you sell. They want to *buy one*, and they want a *great deal*. You have to find a way to make them feel as if doing business with you will save them money, get them a higher quality product, and make their life easier. It has to be all about them (the customer), not you!

<u>Rule 4:</u> Stand out. You can be funny, or extreme in your imagery or situation. Anything that grabs attention. Remember we spoke about even being so odd or "bad" but it resonates in the viewers mind. Making people laugh or question what they just saw can be really useful in grabbing attention. People remember funny or wild. They tell their friends and family about things they see and hear all day.

Final Tips:

- Hard-hitting ending with a great offer can make an impact.
- Use slow motion or anything that interrupts their normal thought pattern and then hit them with the offer after they are drawn in.
- Have a strong and memorable slogan.

Here are some TV Media Buying best practices.

Remember that all four pillars matter. Let's assume you have the creative, and now are looking at what type of programming you want to have your ad placed in.

1. Buy heavy in sports. Most times viewers are not recording these shows to watch later, thus speeding through to skip your commercial because it would be anticlimactic to watch something you already know the outcome of.
2. Really crunch the numbers when buying a spot on a cable channel versus a network channel. I hope you have learned that numbers can be deceiving when emotion gets in the way or if you do not run the full formula. I know it may sound cool that you will be on a prime time network but ego can be an expensive thing.

3. Buy engagement shows and get frequency by buying all of them. An example of engagement show at the printing of this book would be the show *The Big Bang Theory*. People hang on to every word the characters say and hardly ever fast forward through the show. They also watch episode after episode, so you can really get some frequency there. Engagement shows also means viewers pay attention to the show and do not watch it as a second screen or second activity experience.

4. Be careful of highly rated live shows that have limited full engagement. In some cases these are exactly the type of programs people record so they can fast forward to the performances of someone they want to see, sing or dance. If they are fast-forwarding guess what they are skipping: your commercials.

Now let's talk about a few advantages and disadvantages of TV as a medium you should consider for your advertising mix.

Advantage: TV has video and audio, and it is easier to tell a story with the addition of visual effects versus radio that just has audio. It is easier to get people's emotions involved when they use more of their senses.

Disadvantage: You have to really do your homework and follow the formulas I have provided in order to make your other pillars correct. If you do not pay strict attention to this it will be much harder to get the right reach and frequency at a reasonable cost, thus tipping your whole marketing structure.

Radio

Radio is one of the best mediums available today for a small business. Now you may wonder why I would say this but in my opinion it boils down to one thing. Frequency. Most of the time, you cannot get the same frequency on TV for the same money as you can on radio.

I really must pause here to note that there are exceptions. My co-author Tracy Myers is one of these exceptions. He has negotiated a TV buy in his market that allows him to get the same frequency as he would on radio at a cost that makes sense.

Note: When you can get a deal on any medium that will get the reach and frequency you need, at a cost that fits your budget, it doesn't matter what medium you use. In Tracy's case, the CPM, GRPs, reach, and frequency of TV made more sense for him based on his expertly negotiated rates. (See I told you that you would understand these terms. I bet you didn't even flinch)

Here is why it is normally easier to secure frequency on radio. People normally have their car set to four to six stations or the number of pre-set buttons their car has. These four to six stations are what they listen to all the time and have for years. Getting your commercial on one of these stations with the right frequency hits your target audience.

Now a side note because I am sure a few readers are saying they listen to satellite radio and even streaming from your mobile device via Bluetooth (Pandora or Spotify). No doubt each of these have taken a little chunk out of terrestrial radio on the AM/FM dials. Here are some fun facts you want to consider before moving those dollars to the new shiny object that is satellite radio.

1. Satellite or streaming music currently occupies a small chunk of the total market, but terrestrial radio is still the gorilla in the room.
2. Some of your competitors who may be uneducated buyers of media, (not you because you now understand how to buy) have moved the dollars away from regular radio which still works. They have left the door wide open for you to dominate and get a flight of media at a great cost which will lead to a terrific ROI.
3. Stations may be willing to negotiate more than ever due to this defection of buyers.

Here is another point in our discussion of radio versus TV. TV has thousands of stations, and it is much harder to get any kind of loyalty for a TV station than a radio station does. Remember we set our preferred radio stations in our car, you don't channel surf as much on radio as you do on TV.

It really is that simple.

Even if your spot plays more on TV, you may have a harder time getting the same audience six to eight times a week (frequency) for the same dollars as radio. That said, I hope you have remembered that there are tips that I discussed in the TV section about buying the right shows, etc., with engagement that you can use to offset this a little.

Creatively you must cut through the clutter with radio. It is a little harder to do this than on TV because we lose the visual aspect of our creative. I am fairly sure that this is the reason why most auto dealers scream and yell on the radio. They feel that they have to cut through the clutter with volume, and ironically, they become the clutter because we tune them out. They all sound the same.

There is a place for using volume or sound to grab attention and there is also a place to just be different. Tracy Myers and I talk about pattern interrupters all the time when we discuss advertising. Anything that can disrupt the normal patterns of what people hear on the radio can be great if used correctly. Here are some ideas:

1. Slow down your speech. *Like really slow.* Extremes get attention.
2. Dry read. No music in background and minimally produced so it doesn't sound so professionally done.
3. If your market for some odd reason does not have females doing commercials on the radio, use a woman.
4. Use a very unique voice. We use a redneck type of voice in certain markets, and because there is nothing like it on air it stands out.
5. A Ticker-tape sound makes it sound like important news.
6. Catchy slogans that really stick and are easy to repeat.

Let's now talk a little about the creative. Choose your words wisely because it will be the bulk of the creative pillar. Scriptwriting is a skilled profession. It should not be handled by just anyone on your staff or at an agency.

We spoke earlier in the section on TV about Glenn's Why Buy From Me section and it applies here as well. Make sure that your message stands out and no one else can say the same things.

Here are some examples of things that do NOT stand out.

1. We are number 1.
2. Been in business for seventy-five years.

3. Anything that points them to a competitor. Sometimes if the competing business is dominating, a scriptwriter will make an unsuccessful attempt at smearing their competitor and talking about how "We do not do that. We do it another and better way." This makes you look weak.
4. Talking about a price that is not truly a motivator.
5. Any feature that really is standard or everyone already knows about.

What do all of these things have in common? They are all the things that the business owner cares about or feels is important. Not the customer. There is a quote, I am not sure who said it but it goes; "The way to get whatever you want in life is simply give the person who is holding what you want, what they want first.

People want to feel special or that they are getting a good *deal*. One they cannot get anywhere else. Marketing sometimes has to make them beg the question,

"How in the world can they do that"?

If your potential customers wake up Saturday morning with ten choices on where to shop for your product or something similar, you need to have given them a reason to say, "I think we should go check this place out first."

Look at what a big insurance company did with their advertising and business model on both radio and TV.

I am aware I am bringing in a TV example here in the radio section. The point is this. Major Insurance companies break through the clutter with their ads. I want you to strive to give your radio ads as much flavor as this campaign. If you chase this perfection in advertising on the radio, you might just win.

This big insurance company spends millions of dollars to tell you to check their website to see if their rates are lowest. They admit in those advertisements that they may in fact not be the lowest price. So as a consumer, where do you go when you want to shop insurance?

Would you be more inclined to check a website that will compare rates for you, or would you call your local agent to see what their lowest rate is? A big name insurance company bet big that people would use this system they built to give people what they wanted, and therefore, they would sell many more policies to people because they were on their website, not the competitions. (Note: this is a web-based company really, and where do they spend most of their ad money?)

The part that is brilliant about their ads is they also incorporated a funny female character and now a cult phenomenon in her own right. The whole campaign is brilliant from start to finish. It makes you laugh. It interrupts the patterns of normal.

Hopefully you see the major point of sharing this story of a successful ad agency's ad with you. Give people what they want, and they will give you what you want. This was one of the most brilliant moves I have witnessed in all my years advertising.

Let's now share a few rules for your radio spots. You may recognize some similarities from our Rules for TV.

<u>Rule 1:</u> The first six to eight seconds of the commercial has to be engaging. You have to grab attention immediately or else they hit one of their other pre-set buttons.

<u>Rule 2:</u> If you are going to mention reasons to do business with you, make sure your message or claim is unique. We just reviewed your Why Buy message a few pages ago.

<u>Rule 3:</u> No one cares how many you sell. They want to *buy one*, and they want a *great deal*. It has to be all about them (the customer), not you!

<u>Rule 4:</u> Stand out. You can be funny, or extreme in your imagery or situation. The use of funny characters or voices really can stand out here because it will trigger us to picture what this character looks like, and now you have us hooked.

I always say trust your own ear. You listen to radio ads. Now that you are more educated, you will become more of a student of marketing. You will start to notice frequency, good creative and bad creative. Trust yourself. If you like it, so do many other people.

Would you agree that there is a distinct difference between what is blah, uninspiring, "so what," and that others are funny, engaging, and draw you a little more? Listen and make up your own mind.

I want you to commit to me right now. I want you to promise that moving forward, when you sit down to decide your next radio marketing mix that you will never run a "so what" uninspired ad again and waste yours or your company's money!

I am confident after reading this section that you can now have a call your local radio rep and see what it will cost you to run four hundred GRP or sit with your agency now as an informed partner to help put the plan together and write world-class *awesome* creative.

Direct Mail

Direct mail is one of my favorite topics. Let me be clear. Direct mail still works great. I remember my first mailer I sold back in 1992. People asked me then, "How long do you think Direct Mail will last? You should think about what is next in your career because mail is getting saturated, and it won't work this good for long."

They were right to some extent. It stopped working like magic about six years later, but ever since, it has continued to be a workhorse that, when done properly, provides the best ROI of any advertising in large dollar amounts that I can find.

Let's break down direct mail into two of the main players that you need to understand.

Database Mail

Mailing something to customers, with the hope they will open it, can be expensive if done incorrectly. I am sure when a direct mail vendor approached you and delivered their presentation you first reaction may have been "I am not spending that much on a mailer."

Well let's see if we can share some things that may change your mind or prepare you to have a better conversation with that rep the next time.

I feel that Database mail delivers simply the best ROI that any company can invest their marketing dollars into. There really is no substitute for this gem and the reason is simple.

The lists of people you will be contacting are your customers or people who reached out to you. They already know you, like you and hopefully trust you. They know where you are located. They have more than likely been inside your business, feel comfortable with your staff, and can visualize coming back to you.

I feel that many businesses miss out on this form of communication with their existing customer base. They are missing the fact that they have the customer's purchasing or interest history. By using all of this variable data you can personalize your message to them and invite them back to your store for an upgrade, a newer model, service work, browse around at this year's hot merchandise, etc.

Remember you know what they bought, or what they were looking at and if your message is done correctly, you can really appeal to them on a personal level.

An example a variable data mail piece is shown below for the auto industry. As you can see you can speak very personally to a consumer thus they will be more engaged. Imagine if this ad just said, "Hey, you . . . Come in. We are having a sale!" How do you think they would feel versus if you could use all the variables that you have available when you create their message.

< MAIL DATE >

Dear < First >,

The vehicle you are currently driving may actually be worth more today than it was this same time last year.

Pre-owned vehicle values continue to exceed expectations. The high demand for quality, pre-owned vehicles have driven values up by as much as 20%. Inventory at auction houses across the U.S. remain scarce. Simply put, I need your < Year > < Make > < Model > desperately.

When the customer is called by their first name, they are far more likely to keep reading. When you reference the product they own, in this case, the car they just drove home in, they are even more emotionally invested. With this particular mailer, you can even go even further, and are able to tell them what their car is worth. Connection!

There is also a trend where some companies have started to use postcards for mailers like this because they do not have to be opened. My experience has been that if you do something different, maybe if you put a credit-card type card in the envelope attached to the letter they may think it is important and open it. I know from my personal experience, I tend to open these types of mailers just to make sure I am not throwing out a new credit card.

Trying something like this could allow you to send out that more personal type of writing to them versus a colorful and graphically inclined postcard that screams "sale."

Here is a tip for your database customers. Make them feel as if the sale is special to them because of their loyalty and previous business with you. You do not want to make them feel it is a *sale* for everyone.

The second biggest reason why companies do not engage with this type of marketing is they do not have their database in a form they can use. This astonishes me every time. If you have thousands of customers that *know you, like you, trust you, have bought from you,* and *will again if asked,* then why are you treating this list like garbage?

Get your database cleaned and ready to mail at any point. When you think the time is right to use this type of approach, you should have that list fired up and ready to go.

Here is a short list of things to do with your database:

1. Have someone you trust extract the list into a CSV file.
2. Send this file to your mail company to clean it. If you do not have a mail company who can do this, then I would recommend you look into services that can update your records.
3. You should ask the service to de-duplicate the records by address. What you are looking to consolidate is if you have two people in a household that purchased from you, you won't waste the money sending multiple pieces of mail to the same house. It could lose that special feeling or turn them off.
4. You may want to keep the duplicates in a separate list to send them a different looking offer, thus keeping the special feeling going.
5. If you do wholesale business and you do not want to mail other companies, delete all of them or put them in a separate list.
6. If you have the occasional customer that drives from a very far distance (different states, etc.) and you are a retail storefront, delete out-of-state customers.
7. Send all the data through National Change of Address (NCOA).
8. Keep your lists ready to use when you need it.

Some companies ask me if email marketing is better or more cost effective than mailing an actual piece of mail. E-mails are free, and yes, for that reason, they are extremely affordable. But they do not convert like a hard copy piece of mail done correctly.

The idea here is to keep your customers from defecting to another store, another brand, or your competition right across the street. A well thought out piece of mail that makes them feel special may keep them from defecting. It amazes me the dollars that a business will spend to attract a new client but are unwilling to spend correctly to retain their current customer base.

Having your clients defect only means you will have to spend money to bring them back from your competitor.

I am often asked how many times a year should you mail something. That depends on many factors. One of the most important things is the lifecycle of your product. If it is something they need often, like groceries or clothing you may need to mail every month or even weekly.

If you have a product with a longer shelf like an appliance or an automobile, you may have to pay attention to the purchasing cycle. But you can offer things like service or warranty information if you provide these services. My best advice is to sit with a trusted vendor to understand your product and marketing needs to create the right mailing mix.

Saturation Mail

Saturation mail is at the complete opposite end of the spectrum from database mail. As I stated, if database is the best list in the world then saturation mail is the worst. Saturation mail is a piece of mail that is sent to everyone in a certain market whether they are your previous customers or not.

Now if we are looking at our four pillars you may be thinking that this does not fit and why would anyone buy this type of advertising?

There are certain products that do not need a dedicated customer list in order to grab attention. Think of it this way. Is there a car in your driveway? Is there a TV in your home? These big-ticket items are great for using a saturation mail strategy.

That is why you get so many flyers in the mail from electronic stores and car dealerships. That said, it could also work for very high-volume items like pizza shops, grocery stores etc., because everyone eats, and most families shop for food or orders a pizza once in a while. So the goal of this type of marketing is that every house in a desired area is getting hit.

A word of warning! This type of advertising works best if those who receive the mail are close to the location of the company that is mailing them or for online offers.

Let's look at an example of why electronics stores would send you a flyer. The store normally sells many different brands and has a good shot at your business if you are in the market for a TV or something similar. Electronics, like cars, are something people are always looking to show off so if they see something that strikes their fancy, and it has a good price, they may stop in to see it. Remember certain purchases are done on impulse so why not keep in front of the customers face with your ads.

Enter the auto business. They mail their flyer, knowing that not everyone is in the market for a Ford or maybe a Toyota but they bank that enough people, or someone the recipient may know, will be interested in looking at what they have to offer. So in the dealership's mind it is worth saturating the market and inviting everyone in.

In particular, with the auto industry you can be successful with a very small amount of turnout. Sometimes a business can succeed sending out 100,000 of these mailers and get only 100 to150 people to show up for the event. They then measure the resulting sales to justify the cost.

Another reason this type of mail works is because saturation mail can be very inexpensive per piece to send out. You can typically get a large and colorful event-style mailer in each mailbox for less than the cost of a stamp. Saturation has different postage rates because there really is less sorting, etc. Everyone on the mail carrier's route gets one. This is the reason businesses will take this risk. You can get two pieces and sometimes three pieces of saturation type mail for the price of a very targeted mailer in an envelope.

Remember to always refer to your "Why Buy From Me" message when formulating your mail piece.

Here are some quick thoughts on other forms of direct mail, too many to mention without this section getting really lost in the technical aspects and details of each type. I kept this section to database and saturation because they are the opposite ends of the spectrum, and both are very effective because of that.

Other forms of direct mail that you may have heard of or are being sold.

- Conquest mailers. Be careful with these. Many companies want to think they can conquest and steal other companies' customers. In theory, it sounds great. But remember, they know, like, and trust someone else; and they do not know, like, and trust you yet. That alone reduces the response rates dramatically. In my experience, the worst ROI of any mail piece because it takes time to win them over and your message has to be well planned.
- Credit mailers. Many companies send out credit offers. Mostly for cars and credit cards. They do work well if done correctly. I would only caution you on this. Any list of people who should get a credit offer from you may also have been sold to other companies. The danger is that these same customers are getting many similar offers just like yours. It becomes very important for you to stand out with your offer or the response rates will diminish greatly. I would also ask the list vendor if this list has been sold to anyone else in your market. Get it in writing if you can.

- <u>E-mail blasts.</u> Many companies often misuse this form of communication because they view email as free. They just create a mass message (poor creative) and send it to everyone. How does this make anyone in your database feel special? I could write a whole book on this topic but I would recommend doing some research on the right strategy to use email to your advantage versus driving your customers away.

In closing

It has been my goal to put into simple words a few strategies that you can use to make better offline marketing decisions. In many markets Offline Media can be the workhorse that drives the traffic to your online resources and into your place of business.

The thrust of this section was to allow you see the value in offline media. Do you understand how to use it, buy it, and manage it better than ever. I hope that the examples I gave were easy to follow and helpful to show you how the four pillars work together.

More than anything, if you come away from reading this segment with one item hardwired into your brain, it should be this.

You now understand how the four pillars of offline media work.

This knowledge will enable you to now have a great conversation with your vendors to create the right marketing mix. And in my humble opinion if you want to dominate your market, offline media must be a part of your arsenal.

Creating the In-Store Experience by Tracy Myers

If you believe some of the doomsayers, the growth of e-commerce will soon kill off traditional brick-and-mortar stores.

I'm going to show you why you'd be wrong to believe that and why I believe that now is the perfect time for brick-and-mortar stores to begin delivering outstanding and PERSONAL customer experiences to combat the generally ho-hum experiences found in an anonymous digital world.

However, I'm not going to underplay the importance of e-commerce or the direct correlation it's had on the plummeting sales of traditional stores.

Abercrombie & Fitch, Radio Shack, Office Depot and Aeropostale are just a few of the once powerhouse retail stores that have been negatively affected by the rising popularity of ecommerce.

Perhaps the scariest thing to traditional, or offline, business owners is the relatively short period of time it took ecommerce to capture such a sizable market share.

The truth is, you don't even need to be in the retail business to recognize that the way people shop for almost everything now is changing dramatically.

Many traditional offline businesses are closing and others are having to radically change the way they do business.

Most of us just need to look at our own shopping habits and also observe how our main streets and shopping malls look very different to the way they did a few years ago.

Overall, according to the U.S. Census Bureau, e-commerce grew from about two percent of all retail sales to more than six percent over the last ten years.

And these are overall figures so clearly the impact in some areas – such as books and CDs – is much greater.

In recent years, Bureau stats show that ecommerce is growing about three times as fast as traditional retail.

So does this mean we should all give up and accept that we are heading full steam towards a world dominated entirely by online shopping?

NO! While it's true that lots of traditional brick and mortar stores are suffering, they simply need to stop being so TRADITIONAL.

THINK ABOUT THIS:

- Amazon, the 800 pound gorilla of online retailing, is experimenting with retail stores
- Google, the dominant force online, uses physical mail in its marketing and promotions
- Apple, the leading light in latest technology, has retail stores as core to its strategy

Apple, the leading light in the latest technology,
has retail stores as core to its strategy.

The point is that the online shopping experience is important to the economy and to consumers BUT it's not the only game in town.

Brick-and-mortar retail is still a market worth some $4 trillion in the United States.

The fact is that most people would still prefer to do much of their shopping in brick and mortar stores. The problem is very few retailers are giving them a good reason to leave the comfort and convenience of their home to do so. And, even though online shopping will no doubt grow in importance, there's every reason to believe physical stores will continue to play a vital role for successful businesses.

A 2013 study by consultancy firm A T Kearney found that consumers spend the majority of their time shopping in stores (61 percent), followed by online (31 percent), catalog (4 percent) and mobile (4 percent).

Perhaps more important, it found out that the traditional brick-and-mortar stores is the shopping channel of choice across all ages (from millennials to senior citizens) and household income levels (from less than $25,000 per year to more than $100,000 per year).

So my challenge to retailers is not to look at the problems faced by brick-and-mortar stores but to look at the successes some have achieved and look at the opportunities to learn from them.

Some stores are failing because they are sticking to the old approaches but others are succeeding because they are getting it right.

The fact is today's consumers want it all – they live in a world which is now digital, mobile and physical. They are looking for retailers who meet them where they are now and not where they used to be.

They want businesses who can communicate with them and serve them in that mobile, digital, physical world – wherever they happen to be at that moment and whenever they want to do business.

So whatever kind of business you are in, online can play an important role in your marketing and relationship building.

But giving your customers the right in-store experience is what will really determine how much they buy, how often they return and to what extent they act as your salesforce by referring others to you.

In this chapter we'll talk about some of the secrets of making that experience special and making it easy. Here are some of the things we'll cover:

    A. 12 keys to an excellent in-store experience

B. How to ensure the in-store experience matches all your marketing activity
C. Recruit, train and motivate the right people to deliver an excellent experience
D. Key mistakes to avoid with your in-store experience
E. How to make people want to come in to your store
F. 10 steps you can take now to improve your in-store experience

Why You Need an Excellent In-Store Experience

Let's first of all talk about why you need a great in-store experience.

In any business, **people like to deal with people**. While that can work at a distance e.g. over the phone, it usually works best if they deal with people they have actually met in person.

The key advantage of getting people into your stores is that they get to know you – and are therefore more likely to like and trust you – and they get to **build relationships** with you and your staff.

This not only encourages the sale, it **inspires loyalty** and makes them more likely to recommend you to others.

A friend of mine recently wanted to buy a reasonably sophisticated video camera and was quite confused by all the information he found when he started to look online. He realized it was so much easier to go into a local store and talk to one of the staff members there about all the different options available.

A good face-to-face conversation with a sales professional helped him get clear about what he needed and helped them recommend the right option. They actually gave him a guarantee that they'd beat the best price he could find but, for him, saving a few bucks was not the objective. He wanted to find the best solution for his needs and he's now got someone he'll definitely go back to next time he needs something similar.

In contrast to this, the online buying experience is often anonymous so it becomes easy to switch between providers when making any purchase.

When you're shopping online, it's also easy to do a search for the same thing somewhere else before you buy anything.

If you find another retailer selling the same thing cheaper online, you probably won't hesitate to make the switch.

In many industries such as automotive and airline, there are price comparison sites that will help consumers find the cheapest product. The truth is, if you build your business on simply offering the cheapest option, it's not on a very strong foundation.

However if you build it on offering value and back that up with excellent service and an amazing in-store experience, people are not going to go down the road or jump online just to save a few dollars.

An excellent in-store experience builds loyalty and makes people more likely to stay with you.

Another advantage of having people come into your store is that there is automatic **social proof**. People see that others are in the store and buying and hopefully seem to be satisfied.

In my car dealerships, our customer events are a very powerful part of the way we build relationships with customers. Of course, it's the way we serve people on an individual basis that determines the real relationship but it's very important that our customers also feel part of something bigger – that they see others have made the same choice that they have.

In contrast, when making purchases online, people are doing it as individuals and really have no idea what others are thinking.

The whole experience of shopping in-store is very different to shopping online. Going to a store is more of an occasion and can seem more important.

Of course, that's more obvious with bigger purchases but it really applies to everything – even a trip to the grocery store.

I think of it as a little similar to making the choice between going to the cinema and staying home watching movies on the TV. People said technology would kill cinemas and radio but each found ways to adapt and brick-and-mortar retail must do the same.

Another big disadvantage of online commerce is that when people use the Internet, they tend to have a very short attention span and can easily be distracted either to go somewhere else or to do something else entirely.

When you have a consumer in your store, the experience should capture their full undivided attention. That allows you to take the necessary time to help them, give them the information they need and answer their questions without them being distracted.

It's also a great way for you to get to know your customers, their needs and their concerns. So it's one of the best forms of market research.

While the cost of operating an offline store can be more expensive, the profit can also be higher because there is more opportunity to sell the customer additional items. This is called upselling and is easier to do once you have the opportunity to find out what your customers wants and needs are.

Obviously Amazon is a great example of doing this effectively online but there are limits to how well technology can understand customers. When you have the opportunity to get to know someone, you have more chance of helping them identify other ways you can meet their needs.

One of the big worries that people have when buying online is what they will do if something goes wrong or if they have a complaint. A big advantage of brick-and-mortar is that people have the sense that there is somewhere they can go and someone they can talk to for personal service rather than being stuck sending an email or being transferred to someone at a call center disguised as a customer service department.

That's a big advantage that offline retailers should exploit more.

Of course, none of that is to suggest that online isn't important and shouldn't play an important role in most businesses.

But there are many advantages to having a strong in-store experience and making it as powerful as possible.

A. 12 Keys to an Excellent In-store Experience

So we've talked about why the in-store experience is important.

Now let's talk about some of the key elements that make in-store special and how you can take advantage of each of them.

1. Customers have direct contact with products
2. Shopping can be an enjoyable experience
3. You can provide personalized expert advice
4. Shopping is done in company of other people
5. You can appeal to all the senses
6. Opportunity to build relationships

7. Immediate gratification
8. After sales care
9. Shopping experience can be shared
10. Opportunities for upsell and value-added
11. Events and occasions
12. Commitment made to time spent

1. Customers have direct contact with products

One of the most significant benefits for people being able to shop in a brick and mortar store is that they can see, touch and smell the product they want to buy.

That's why it's so important that the overall experience you provide in-store makes people want to buy from you while they are there and come back to you when they need more of what you have.

2. Shopping can be an enjoyable experience

When people go to make purchases online, it's natural for them to feel overwhelmed by all the choices they have in front of them. Perhaps they feel a little rushed because they are attempting to make the purchase during their lunch break at work or maybe they are feeling stressed because their kids are yelling at each other in the background. Regardless, that's part of the way online shopping works and it's completely natural.

That's why it's imperative that brick-and-mortar stores make their shopping experience positive and memorable. It encourages the customers to stay longer which entices them to buy more.

When the experience is positive, people will want to stay longer and are therefore more likely to buy more. It makes it something that people want to repeat and share with others – so they will not only come back, they will also tell their friends about it.

If you are delivering an experience that makes customers want to come back and also makes them encourage others to visit you, you are well on your way to building strong and positive long-term customer relationships.

The challenge you need to meet if you want to make the most of this opportunity is to do what you can to make the process of shopping easy, enjoyable and FUN. Try to ensure it is memorable and is something people want to repeat.

3. You can provide personalized expert advice

One of the benefits of shopping in a physical store is being able to talk to knowledgeable employees about all of the available options.

Well-trained staff members will ask the right questions and provide information that can help customers have greater confidence when making buying decisions.

When buying certain products, customers are not always aware of all the different options available and they value someone who can provide them with the information they need to make an informed decision.

You can make the most of this by ensuring your staff are knowledgeable about your products and able to ask questions so that they get to understand what the customer is looking for without seeming too pushy. After all, there is a HUGE difference in selling and telling. Customers like being sold but none of us like to be told.

4. Shopping is done in company of other people

When you shop in a physical store, you will normally be surrounded by other people.

Of course this can be a disadvantage if the store is busy and people feel they are not getting the attention they wanted.

Please know that while your customer should never be ignored, there is something that I like to call the empty restaurant effect. No one likes to eat at in an empty restaurant. In fact, most people will go to a busy restaurant and wait to eat before they'll stop to eat in an empty one? Why? It's psychological. If the restaurant is busy, customer assume it's a great place to eat and must be worth the wait. The opposite holds true for the empty one.

People are more likely to buy when they are surrounded by other people buying and this may draw their attention to purchases they hadn't otherwise considered.

You can also see this happening at a very basic level in the grocery store. People often go in with a clear idea of what they want, see someone else pick something up off a shelf or see it in their shopping basket and think, "I must try that."

Very often it's when you see someone else pick something up off a shelf or you see it in their shopping basket that you think, "I must try that."

The exact same process works with larger and more complex purchases. When customers see what other customers are buying, it makes them check out those options as well.

This works both on a conscious and unconscious level.

You can make the most of this by ensuring that you have a staff that is trained to pick up on these buying signs, and by creating an environment where everyone feels relaxed and happy.

5. You can appeal to all the senses

The decision making process is very rational when people shop online. They tend to only look at features, read reviews and compare prices.

When you shop in a store, you are much more open to being influenced by other sensory experiences.

First, there is clearly the ability to see and touch the products as we discussed. However, you will also be influenced by other sensory aspects including the sounds around you and the smell in the store.

Factors such as being able to look a salesperson in the eye, shake their hand and listen to what they're saying caters for many more of the senses than a pure online transaction and therefore helps build trust.

One of the ways you can take advantage of this is making sure that your store appeals to all of the senses – it looks good, smells nice (whether that's perfume or the smell of cookies or coffee), sounds attractive e.g. with appealing music and overall it's a pleasant environment.

6. Opportunity to build relationships

When people come in to your store, you have the opportunity to build relationships with them that are more difficult to achieve online.

People might find it convenient to shop at online stores such as Amazon but they rarely feel any bond or connection with those retailers. You need some element of personal contact to build a strong relationship and the strongest of all is when that happens face to face.

When someone comes into your store, you can still get many of the benefits that you would get from an online transaction. For example, you can still collect their email address and use it to communicate with them later.

If you have effective customer relationship management systems, you can use those to keep track of who are your most important customers and treat them accordingly.

All of that can be done through technology and works regardless of the sales channel you are using.

However, it seems as if most brick and mortar stores have forgotten that they have a huge advantage over online stores. This advantage existed way before ecommerce did and it is one of the success secrets that my family has believed in for 85 years...going back to when my great grandfather when he opened the first Frank Myers store. This advantage is PEOPLE, the relationships they can build with customers and the excellent experience they can help provide. Sadly, it seems that people have also become a disadvantage in a lot of businesses but that MUST change in order for brick and mortar stores to survive moving forward.

7. Immediate gratification

One of the big reasons people want to shop in a brick-and-mortar store is they can often walk away faster with the product they have purchased.

When you order online, you have the inconvenience of having to wait for your product to be delivered... a product you've often never seen, touched, tried on or tried out in person. Of course, services like Amazon prime are expediting orders to arrive the same day. That's why it's more important than ever for traditional stores to offer an extraordinary experience for their customers.

That can be as simple as the packaging you use to let them take away their purchase or it can perhaps be bonuses or extra gifts you use to make it more memorable.

Always remember that "buyer's remorse" can set in fairly quickly after buying so the ability to be there in person to secure the deal can have many advantages.

8. After-sales care

While many people are attracted to the advantages of buying online, a big disadvantage is the worry about what they should do when things go wrong.

On one level, that may be as simple as something not being quite right for you. For example, you buy a shirt online and it's not quite the right size or the color is not exactly the way it looked on the website.

You now have to go through all the hassle of sending it back and waiting for the replacement to arrive – then hoping they get it right second time around.

However it can be a major issue when the laptop you bought stops working after just three months and you need it today to do your work. So you have to work out how you are going to get the problem solved quickly enough.

The big advantage of the in-store experience is that people can get fast attention when they have problems. This can work particularly well if you are offering both online and offline sales channels.

One way to make best use of this is to emphasize the importance of after sales service to your customers whether they buy from you online or in-store.

9. Shopping experience can be shared

For many purchases, the decision can involve several people – perhaps a couple buying something together, a whole family involved in a decision or someone simply taking advice from a friend.

While it's true two people can sit down at a computer together and look at the options, going to a store is much more of a shared experience and therefore one that may well create a higher chance of purchase.

People often feel more confident in their purchase when there is someone else around so are more willing to buy. And there is someone else there to reassure them when any signs of buyer's remorse start to arise.

A shared experience is also often more pleasurable which in and of itself makes someone more likely to make a decision to buy.

You can take advantage of this by ensuring that your in-store experience makes it easy for people to shop together which in some cases may involve providing facilities for children or for people to sit down and have a cup of coffee together.

10. Opportunities for upsell and value-added

When someone comes into your store, there are many opportunities for them to become aware of other products you have available and for you to talk about those.

In the first place, they are likely to see things in your store that they didn't know about – or didn't know that you sold.

They will also see what other people are buying and that will open up new ideas for them that they hadn't considered previously.

And, of course, you get a chance to get to know them and suggest other things to them.

This partly comes about because you can suggest appropriate solutions to them but is also a factor of the trust you and your team are able to develop through getting to know them in person.

Clearly, this can also work online but perhaps in a more limited way.

The A T Kearney study I mentioned earlier found that 40 percent of consumers spend more money than they had planned in stores, while only 25 percent reported online impulse shopping.

It follows that strategies that drive consumers to stores – whether it is to shop or pick up a product purchased online – will encourage more impulse purchases.

One way to take advantage of this fact is to make sure that people have a reason for coming to your physical location rather than doing everything through online or direct delivery.

Another thing is, once someone comes into your location, find reasons for them to go into other parts of your store as well as the one they may have specifically come to.

11. Events and occasions

When you have a brick and mortar store, you have a great opportunity to give people a reason to visit other than to simply buy. This may be special promotional events or customer appreciation events and it is an important part of building relationships and trust.

One way to take advantage of this is to ensure you have regularly held special events taking place that customers and potential customers are invited to.

As I mentioned before, this is something that is really important to me in my car dealerships and is a vital way that we build and grow our relationships with our customers. It's something we do for specific events such our community wide Trunk or Treat in the Fall, our community appreciation picnic that we have in the Spring or something that we do at various times during the year such as a supporting the Christmas Toy Drive to benefit the Salvation Army.

The key is not necessarily to look at an event and see how many sales you make but to make it part of the way that you get to know your customers and build stronger relationships with them.

12. Commitment made to time spent

When someone comes into your store, they have already made a commitment of time that indicates they are seriously interested in buying.

The more time they spend, the more often they come back and the more likely they are to buy.

On the other hand, visiting a website may only last a few seconds.

Psychologist Robert Cialdini, author of the book "Influence" identified commitment as one of the key principles involved in the persuasion process.

Once you can get someone to take a small step, they will be more likely to take the next bigger one.

That means simply by spending time in your store, someone is already making a commitment to you and is therefore more likely to buy.

You can take advantage of this by giving people incentives to spend more time in your store – perhaps because it's a pleasant experience or by giving them reasons to come back more often.

B. How to ensure the in-store experience matches all your marketing activity

Of course, in talking about all the advantages of in-store experiences, I'm not saying that any retailer should avoid also providing an online offer.

These days, for most businesses, consumers expect you to be able to serve them in the way that suits their needs best.

There are some people who prefer to deal online and there are some people prefer to be offline. But often many people like to use both – either for different purposes or at different times.

That means the key to success is ensuring that your in-store expedience is consistent with what you are doing online and with your offline advertising.

Here are some ways you can make this work to best effect.

Ensure consistency

People will often approach your business in different ways and that's why it's important to ensure that you have consistency in the way you look and in the tone you use to communicate with people.

If people see you online, a TV commercial or even direct mail, you should look like the same business that you do when they come into your store.

It's not too surprising that the experience of going in to an Apple retail store is consistent with what you experience of Apple in other media. But so many people seem to think there's a certain way you need to look online and a different way you appear in physical locations.

Increasingly the same people see you in many different media and that experience has to be consistent if you don't want to cause confusion and disconnect.

You don't have to have a big budget to do that. Small touches such as having photos of your store not only on your website but also on your social media profiles as well as in your offline marketing can make a major impact. For example, I am the spokesperson for my dealerships so my photo is consistent across all of my marketing platforms.

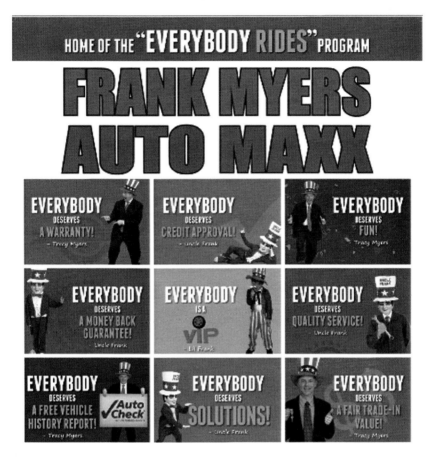

Since I am the spokesperson for my dealerships,
I have my photo on both the website and the Facebook page.
This ties my brand and my marketing message together.

Be aware of the role of each channel

Sometimes it helps to be aware that people will approach your business in different ways for different purposes.

This depends on the products and services you offer and the way you choose to work.

However you want to make sure that it's all integrated so for example people can order things from you online and collect in your store.

The reality is that many purchases involve various stages starting with research, followed by testing then purchase followed by pick-up or delivery and ending with after-sales experience.

Each channel can play a different role. Digital channels are often most important at the research stage where people check out information online, read reviews and seek recommendations through social media. The physical store may be more important in other stages.

Here are some of the ways the different channels can be integrated:

- Order online and pick up in the store to collect
- Buy in-store and then go to a website to watch a how-to-use video
- Go in-store to get more information about something seen online
- Go to an in-store event for training on how to use a product bought online

Drive from offline to online and back to offline

One of the most exciting opportunities in retail is the potential for greater integration between online and offline.

This is built on the realization that the success of one doesn't have to be to the detriment of the other.

Indeed, there is even a buzzword created to name this phenomena - O2O. It means "Online to Offline".

This is broadly about using online marketing methods to drive people to your physical location.

However, rather than seeing it as a one step process, I see it as a more fluid process.

In the first step, you use traditional marketing to drive people to your website and other online locations so that you can start to build the relationship.

Then, having collected their details, your website and email marketing activity is focused on the next step, which is encouraging people to come into your store so keeping them informed about new releases and special offers for example.

After that, even if people are coming into your store regularly, you want to make sure you have a way of communicating with them online.

Naturally, you probably want to communicate with them offline as well but email is a cheap, fast and easy way to communicate – especially giving details of special offers.

Use online to enhance your service

People may want to come in to your store to make a purchase but don't necessarily want to come in every time they need something so make sure you have ways that they can go to an online resource that will help them.

For example, they should be able to visit your website to get information about your current offers and hours of operation. If they need to discuss a complicated issue, they may prefer to visit the store.

While this is usually the most convenient option for the customer, it has the benefit of helping to minimize the retailer's costs as well.

Use social media

In today's marketplace, social media is an extremely valuable way to keep in touch with your customers, build relationships and encourage them to share information about you with others.

This can be particularly powerful if you have a business that doesn't involve frequent contact with customers in a way – for example it is an occasional purchase.

It's not just about having a token presence but is about making the most of the opportunity to stay in front of customers in a way that doesn't require them to make a purchase.

The exact way to use social media varies between businesses and depends on how much time you want to commit to it but here are ten examples of ways you can use social media in your retail business:

1. Use your Facebook Page to show customers a touch of your personal side
2. Use Twitter to publish news announcements about your own products and offers and also news relevant to your market
3. Run surveys of customers and prospective customers
4. Advertise your store – especially offers and events – using the tools to target potential customers very directly
5. Set up a Twitter account to handle support questions
6. Encourage customers to refer you to their friends
7. Set up a customer-only Facebook page and give them special offers
8. Encourage reviews on sites such Google or Yelp
9. Reach out to potential customers and influencers in your area or market based on their stated location or interests
10. Monitor what is happening in your market and what key issues interest people.

One of the key things about social media is that it does require a bit of time commitment if you are going to do it properly.

For example, you need to respond to comments – especially anything negative – really quickly.

It helps connect you with people when the connection can't always be face to face.

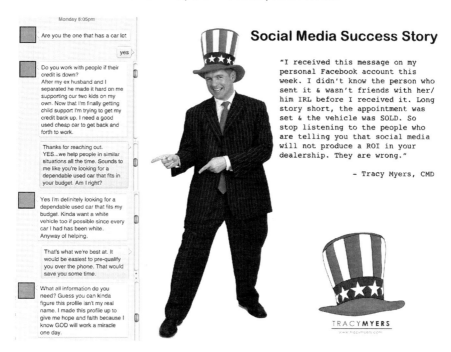

Social Media Success Story

"I received this message on my personal Facebook account this week. I didn't know the person who sent it & wasn't friends with her/him IRL before I received it. Long story short, the appointment was set & the vehicle was SOLD. So stop listening to the people who are telling you that social media will not produce a ROI in your dealership. They are wrong."

– Tracy Myers, CMD

Capture information to get to know your customers better

You want to build as broad picture of your customers as possible so that you can communicate with them in the most appropriate way.

A key element of this is having the right customer relationship management system so that you can keep track of your customers and the contact you have with them at an individual level.

You want to be able to communicate by email, snail mail, telephone or even text, depending on the needs and circumstances.

But you also want to be able to communicate according to where they are in their relationship with you. The communication to a new prospect is very different to the communication with someone who has been with you 25 years.

A VIP customer needs a very different message than someone who just buys small amounts occasionally.

Having the right CRM system allows you tailor the message appropriately online, offline and in-store.

Use multi-channel marketing campaigns to support each other

Just a few short years ago, consumers received the majority of their marketing messages from the "Big 3" forms of traditional media: TV, radio and newspaper.

That has changed drastically because media is now extremely fragmented. Consumers are bombarded with marketing messages everywhere they turn. It's gotten so competitive that there was an ad talking to me from the bottom of a urinal at the airport last week. This type of marketing fragmentation also makes it more difficult for businesses to get their message heard and seen through all of the clutter. In addition, streaming services like Netflix, Amazon Prime Video, Sirius satellite radio and Apple iTunes radio have made media available without any commercials while DVR's make it easier than ever to fast forward through the ads.

So now what? Getting your marketing message heard by consumers is not nearly as difficult as I may have made it seem. However, to quote the great Bob Dylan, "the times they are a-changin'".

Businesses must use multi-channel marketing campaigns instead of just relying on offline, or traditional media, like they did in years past. For example, your TV commercial may drive the consumer to text their number to receive a 15% off coupon. The coupon gets sent to their phone with a link to sign up to receive another 5% off. To get the bonus 5%, the consumer must enter a valid email address which goes directly to the businesses CRM. The CRM should have a sequence of follow-up emails scheduled to go out to the consumer and should be customized to so they directly relate to the offer that was initially responded to.

Most importantly, the in-store experience should match ALL of the correspondence up to this point. If your message, music, colors and images are fun then that is what the consumer should see once they arrive in-store. This is where most businesses fail miserably and where YOU can stand out from crowd.

Use one media to support another

These days many customers expect retailers to be available where and when they need them and not just through one channel or another.

That means, for example, someone may place an order through an app on their smartphone but we want to come in to your store to pick it up or to get further information about how best to use it.

Your in-store experience needs to be at the core of that offer.

C. Recruit, train and motivate the right people to deliver an excellent experience

For most retail businesses, one of the keys to delivering an excellent in-store experience is how successful you are at recruiting, training and motivating the right people to deliver it.

Part of that comes down to hiring the right people in the first place and that's often where people make a mistake.

Here's my 7-point plan for making this element work:

1. Recruit for Personality

People are often put into roles in a business because of their technical knowledge or because of their previous job experience. This may work in some industries, such as being a Doctor, but hiring like this can be setting someone up for failure. I've found that one of my secrets to hiring the right people is to choose the right kind of personality. You can train most other things but it can be difficult to train someone to have the right personality to effectively handle customers. You want to recruit people who know how to build relationships and understand customers.

2. Reward Sales Effort

Make certain they have a willingness to sell. In many roles, it's important to take into account the person's willingness to encourage customers to make the purchase. It's also important to know that it's not just about ensuring the person spends money with the business before they leave but also to consider that the customer was underpromised, overdelivered and overwhelmed with an amazing in-store experience. As I've said, finding someone with the right personality is important. It's not just about making friends and having a nice conversation. It's also about making sure the customer signs on the line that is dotted AND leaves happy that they gave you their hard earned money. A great sales person sees themselves as a Solutions Provider. They are on the side of the customer, they LISTEN to what they need, they work diligently to obtain the best solution to meet their needs AND they bend over backwards to guarantee that the in-store experience is so good that they feel the need to tell EVERYONE about it.

3. Provide Effective Scripts and Training

One of the most important things that determines the really successful customer experience is ensuring that people have the right training and – most important – scripts to deliver the outcomes required. If you look at the really successful businesses like Disney or even McDonald's, they have thought about every scenario and provided people with the right scripts to use in every situation.

In a fast food restaurant, it's as simple as an upsell question like, "Would you like fries with that?" Big theme parks are one of the world's great examples of effective customer service and giving the customer a great experience. One of the key elements in that success is that they have developed a very detailed range of scripts that people use in different situations to ensure the customer goes home happy and wants to return as soon as possible. Scripts are not just about what people say on the telephone when they are trying to sell. Effective scripts help in everyday situations by ensuring the employee knows exactly how to deal with the customer in a way that will satisfy them. That process may seem like hard work – and it is a lot of work to establish scripts. But you don't need to do them all at once and think of the enormous amount of time and frustration saved each time someone doesn't have to waste time working out what to say to a customer in a specific situation.

4. Incentivize the Success You Want

In many retail businesses, an important part of the process of motivating staff is ensuring they have some form of direct reward for their own success. Creating the right kind of compensation structure can be complicated as you don't want to create division and you don't want to encourage inappropriate sales.

But getting this right can make a big difference to the profits of the business and customer satisfaction.

Rewards can be given for a number of different reasons – overall profit, individual sales made or customer satisfaction scores, for example. And they can apply at the individual level or to the team overall, or a mixture of both. The key is to identify what behavior and results you want to encourage and find a way to do that successfully.

5. Encourage Teamwork

In delivering excellent customer experience – and increased sales – there are very often a number of people involved.

The overall success of the retail experience can depend just as much on the politeness of the delivery driver as on the sales skills of person in-store. Overall success demands a variety of different skills and a range of different people are therefore often involved.

It's not just about the people making the sale, it's also about the people who make the sale stick and provide reasons for customers to come back. Each stage of the process may involve different people.

In order to maximize success, you need to create a culture of teamwork so that people support each other and share their experience of what works.

People need to recognize the importance of working together to give the customer a great experience.

Again that's something where big theme parks are a great role model. Everybody is a "cast member" whether it's the shop assistants, the people who keep the place clean or the technicians who make sure everything works.

Everyone knows they are part of a team and has pride in the role they play of delivering a memorable experience for their visitors.

6. Hire Slow and Fire Fast

Your people are such an important part of your success, so it's important to devote the right time and attention to getting the recruitment process right. Too often this happens because we are in a hurry. We need someone yesterday. Nevertheless, we can operate recruitment in a way that gives us time to make the right decisions, to find people who fit in with our culture and have the right personal qualities and skills. Virtually every person in a retail business can in some way help create a great customer experience or can ruin it. Obviously people make mistakes and you need to give them the right support and training but the most expensive mistake you can make could be putting the wrong person in front of a customer.

7. Go the Extra Mile

One thing I look for in recruiting staff is finding people who are willing not just to do what is expected of them but to go the extra mile to help the customer and to encourage the success of the business. Of course, that needs to be reasonable. You don't write blank checks to give things away. But I can think of many examples where I have seen – both as a retailer and a customer – a single employee doing something they didn't need to do to help the customer.

I've seen employees using their own time to help a customer solve a problem that wasn't directly related to what we were offering but was important to the customer. I've had people coming in early to help me sort out an issue that I couldn't do at any other time. These are all indications that part of the effective retail experience is making the whole process positive and memorable for the customer. It's a cliché, I guess, but we should always treat our customers the way we would want to be treated ourselves in the same situation.

D. Key mistakes to avoid with your in-store experience

Let's have a look now at some of the mistakes many businesses make that stop them from delivering the excellent in-store experience.

Not making customer convenience the priority: If you want your customers to have an excellent experience, you need to make it as easy as possible for them to do business with you. That may mean a free home delivery service, extended hours or maybe a 24-hour customer service hotline.

Cutting corners on people: All businesses have to maximize their bottom line and that means cutting out unnecessary costs but sometimes savings can be false. If you don't have enough staff, customers get frustrated and don't come back.

If your staff is not properly trained and equipped with the right scripts and knowledge, customers are either disappointed or sales are not what they could be. Cutting back on giving your staff the right training will save money today but can destroy future growth and profits.

If you don't have enough staff, customers get frustrated and don't come back. If staff are not properly trained and equipped with the right scripts and knowledge, customers are either disappointed or sales are not what they could be.

Cutting back on giving your staff the right training and motivation can be a false economy.

Blaming others on the team: For customers to have a great experience, the team has to be working together to give them that experience. However sometimes things can go wrong.

People on the team should never blame others within the team for that. Everyone has equal responsibility to create a great experience and sort out problems.

Failing to anticipate problems: We can all tend to assume that things have been set up properly but often the unexpected happens.

We need to take time to anticipate whether there could be problems and how we handle those problems when they arise so that wherever possible the problem is solved before the customer realizes.

Not looking outside of own industry: Too often look for inspiration within our own industry and at our own industry and at our competitors rather than outstanding successes in other fields.

If you want to provide excellent experience look to the people in other markets that provide an excellent experience and see what you can learn from them.

Failing to turn complaints into opportunities: When things don't go as expected, most customers are only looking for a solution.

If we're not ready to give customers the solution that they are looking for then they will be disappointed and their experience will be tarnished.

Too much automation: The keys to the successful in-store experience are providing the personal touch and building relationships.

In many other areas of business, we have come to rely on automation – impersonal emails for example.

We need to be ready to ensure that the personal touch comes across with the in-store experience.

E. 10 steps you can take now to improve your in-store experience

Let's now take a look at some of the steps you can take right away to create even more effective in-store experiences.

1. Develop and Use Scripts OR "Why Buy From Me" Statement

By now, it should be obvious how important I feel that scripts are in order to maximize the success of a business. Not only can they empower your Team Members by telling them exactly what to say in uncomfortable situations but they can also make your customer feel more at ease when their questions or problems are handled quicker and more efficiently. Don't be overwhelmed by the somewhat daunting task of writing scripts. Simply identify some of the most important interactions that your customers have with your Team Members and write down what should be said in each of these situations. An example might be when someone comes in with a complaint. Team Members are often unsure how to handle these situations. Instead of them having to find a Manager to resolve the issue and having the customer to wait (which is the WORST thing that can happen), give them the exact words to use.

2. Identify and Share Your Unique Positioning Statement OR "Why Buy From Me" Statement

Develop a Unique Positioning Statement, sometimes called a Why Buy From Me statement, which is a list of reasons why consumers should do business with you and not your competition. Then look for ways to promote your statement in your store such as through video, point of purchase displays and even on merchandise. What you're trying to do is set yourself apart from your competition and make the transaction about more than a commodity.

As a side note, Team Members should ALWAYS know what the stores Unique Positioning Statement is. Knowing it and sharing it with customers should be part of the culture.

3. Improve Signage

Part of an excellent in-store experience is that people should easily be able to find what they want.

Try to see it from the viewpoint of someone who's never visited your store before. Hire people to come in and give you feedback on how easy it is to find their way around and help you identify changes you need to make.

Good signage should also be used to identify current specials or offers as well as pointing out where to park or where the restrooms are.

4. Develop a Loyalty Program

A loyalty program encourages people to do what the name implies...be loyal to your store. Loyalty can be measured by how much people buy but it can also be measured by how often they visit. For example, a frozen yogurt store may have a loyalty card that offers buy 5 cones and get the 6th cone free. An automotive service department could offer a free car wash with every oil change when the customer uses their loyalty card. Something as simple as a free cup of coffee can play a role in encouraging people to come back more often and spend more while they are there.

5. Develop VIP Experiences

My dad, affectionately known as Uncle Frank, always said: "Your customer will pay almost anything if you give them an experience they will remember."

Amen!

Creating fun events or activities that entice people to visit your store will also quickly help them become your customers. For example, one of the car dealerships that I consult for has a "What To Expect" workshop for all new customers. They are invited to a local restaurant, they are fed, introduced to the dealerships Director Of Service and sent home with a handful of coupons for the service department. It doesn't cost a lot to do but it has become a powerful customer relationship tool.

Another fun idea is Family Movie Night where families are invited to your store to watch a new release while you offer free refreshments like popcorn and pizza.

At one of my car dealerships, we take our customers photo on a Red Carpet when they buy a car. This makes them feel like a celebrity by giving them a VIP Experience that they'll never forget.

How about offering something that makes your customers feel luxurious like free valet parking or having on on-site masseuse? Create something that makes people want to come to your store – whether it's a game room, live music, coffee bar, library or a photo booth. It doesn't really matter as long as you find fun things that will appeal to people of all ages.

As a side note, remember to cater to your customer base. For example, you probably wouldn't offer a knitting class if your primary customer base is made up of millennials.

6. Emphasize Free Advice

As we already discussed, the ability to get personal advice is a major reason why the in-store experience is still really important.

You can emphasize the importance of this by demonstrating to people that they're welcome to come in and get advice even if they are not ready to purchase.

Hardware stores Lowes and Home Depot are both masters of this. They offer free home improvement workshops for things such as brick laying, faux painting, drywall repair and many others.

7. Make It Easy

You need to make it easy for people to do business with you. This may be something as simple as looking at the hours you are open.

Consider whether the days and hours you are open are right for your customers. Consider an extension of your regular hours, opening special hours for certain occasions or possibly even opening on days that you are currently closed.

How about offering a free shuttle service, a free delivery service or offering a 24 hour customer service department?

For better or for worse, we're living in a NOW society. Your goal should be to make it easier to do business with you than with your competition.

8. Offer more upsells

Always be thinking about ways in which you can encourage people to make additional purchases or even to consider purchases in completely different areas. Identify some specific products or packages you can use as part of this process.

9. Improve or change your hours of operation

Consider whether the days and hours you are open are right for your customers. Consider an extension of your regular hours, opening special hours for certain occasions or possiblyeven opening on days that you are currently closed.

10. Create a unique experience

Create something that makes people want to come to your store – whether it's a game room, live music, coffee bar, library or a photo booth. It doesn't really matter as long as you find fun things that will appeal to people of all ages.

A photo booth can be an inexpensive and fun way to help create a memorable experience for your customers.

Seizing the Opportunity

The role of physical retail stores is changing as people get more used to purchasing in a range of different ways, including digital and mobile.

It's clear that those changes mean we need to think differently about the in-store experience so that we can use it build better relationships and bonds with customers.

Writing about this reminds me of a story that my great grandpa told my dad about two men who owned little country stores across the road from each other about 85 years ago. One man was a Mr. Roy Black and one was Mr. B. They both sold ice cream. They both charged the same amount for their ice cream. Their stores looked about the same in appearance. They were both good people. But there were always twice as many people at Roy Black's store than Mr. B's store. Why, you might ask?

When you went into Mr. B's store he would ask, "Hello, what can I get for you?" When you told him "ice cream," he proceeded to get it for you, hand it to you, tell you how much it cost, take your money, say "thank you", and off you went.

When you went into Roy Black's store he asked, "Hey, how are you today? How is your family? Isn't it a beautiful day? How can I help you?"

You would tell him you wanted ice cream, and he would tell you all the different flavors he had and ask you if you wanted to sample one. Then he would proceed to make you an ice cream cone and offer you a chair to sit down while you stayed a little while, ate your ice cream, and talked with him. If you had children with you, he would even sit them in his lap while they ate theirs and he talked with you.

When you were ready to leave, he would thank you, get up from his chair, and walk you to the door to say 'goodbye'. When you got in the car he would wave goodbye to you and say, "Come back to see me," and you would, of course. Who wouldn't when they were treated so cordially?

Mr. B offered you ice cream but Roy Black offered you ice cream and an "experience." It was an experience that my Great Grandpa remembered all of his life and passed on to my dad who passed it on to me.

I am fortunate to have learned the life lesson and simple business model of Roy Black and I believe there is plenty of evidence that supports creating a powerful instore experience like his will be vital for many retailers to give them an edge over their competitors.

However, those who really succeed will be the ones who master all three elements we are discussing in this book – the online, the offline and the in-store.

Now What?

After reading these last three chapters/segments on online media, offline media, and the in-store experience, I would think your head might be spinning. I can imagine business owners or marketing managers just sitting in a room and saying, "Now what?"

Let me share some good news that might allow you to breathe again. There is no perfect answer. There are many different ways for you to utilize your budget, and like a living organism, your marketing efforts will and should always be evolving and changing. In simple terms, there is no "right" answer.

Every market is different. Every industry is different. Every budget is different. Every leader's stomach for change is different. Every vendor partner is different. Your education level is different than your competition.

That said; there is a right approach. There is a right attitude toward a Connected Marketing Strategy, and there certainly could be catastrophic results if you just blindly start to spend money on things you think you should try. The goal for this closing segment is to help you get on the right track and make some educated and connected decisions on your approach toward your overall marketing strategy.

Here are the items we will be covering to help you make the best use of what you have learned and turn the reading you have just done into actionable items:

1. Overall strategy vs. Individual Silos
2. Comfort Zone for Change
3. Resources and Time
4. Connect
5. Measure

1. Overall strategy vs. Individual Silos

You just read three segments on online media, offline media, and in-store experience. It could be very easy to take one section and then apply those strategies, especially if you understand them better than some of the other sections.

If you take anything away from this book, it should be that there are no individual silos in your business. Everything is connected. From your marketing to the interaction with your team to the interaction with your customers, moving one piece without understanding the impact on other departments will negatively impact your results.

The first thing to do is sit with your team and map out what you are currently doing. What marketing efforts are being done offline, online and then in-store. Before we can adjust, we need to know where we stand.

Create a simple spreadsheet listing types of marketing, the current budget, if you are using specific phone numbers or ways to track the campaigns, do the campaigns direct to a specific page on the website, who handles the calls or leads etc. Once you have this information, then you can begin to use this book to make adjustments.

Under no circumstances does anything get changed without everyone who handles marketing or customer engagement is at the table.

For example if your offline agency is creating a new radio campaign, as we discussed in the book, your online marketing agency should speak with them to tell them where to direct traffic on the website, or to give them a specific tracking phone number so you can monitor results.

If you are increasing your online marketing spend in order to increase phone calls and lead forms (which all businesses love) then you need to discuss this change with the people who will handle the calls and leads to make sure they are prepared.

Understand that looking at the ROI of one silo is not effective because all of these efforts are connected and affect your overall ROI/results.

2. Comfort Zone for Change

Every business leader, when they look in the mirror understands their comfort zone for change. Some leaders run very lean and are risk averse. Others seem like gamblers ready to outspend their competition.

Why I want to discuss your comfort zone is because many of these topics we discussed in these three sections, you may not fully understand. I applaud your reading the book in order to educate yourself, but now thinking of where to begin or what to apply may push against your comfort zone.

My advice is to go slow. Decide on one aspect or area that you think you would like to investigate. Get the right people/ vendors to the table so you feel more comfortable with the decision. Next you will have to decide if you spending additional money on this venture or re-allocating existing funds.

Either way, set a clear budget with your vendor or team, set clear expectations of what results you are looking for. Do not be afraid to ask your vendor how long it will be before you see results.

Lastly, make sure that if you are re-allocating funds you see how taking money from one area may impact its performance. Remember everything is connected.

3. Resources and Time

Now that you have decided on your approach and budget for this endeavor, you need to make sure you have enough in the budget that allows the campaign to run for a certain period of time. Too often there is a knee jerk reaction to cancel or change course if results are not seen immediately. There are some online marketing campaigns or in-store processes that should show quick results but as I mentioned, make sure you are discussing what results you can expect with your vendor.

Note: If your campaign requires additional staff to handle the increase in leads or calls have them trained and in place before launching the campaign. You cannot judge the success of the campaign if the connected part is not functioning as well.

4. Connect you Marketing

Now that you are embracing Connected Marketing, you will need to make sure that all of your agency partners are using consistent assets.

Some of the items that should be reviewed for consistency are:

1. Logo: Colors, sizes, etc.
2. Taglines or slogans
3. Themes or characters

Remember our goal is to connect our message in a consistent way, no matter where our customers find us.

How effective will your marketing continue to be if customers see different themes, colors etc. on different connection points?

Note: When you are beginning to log all of your marketing on your spreadsheet, a good idea would be to have copies of all of the assets you are using in your Offline-Online or In-Store marketing. It will help you to see if there are any gaps in consistency and also allow all of your vendors to have feedback in a Connected Marketing Solution.

I implore you to hold your agency or in-house marketing director (yourself) to a higher standard when it comes to your creative.

If your ads resemble white space on TV or get lost with a monotonous one-tone voice on radio, maybe have poorly written ads on Google AdWords, or just do not stand out when they get to the website do not spend the money. Your goal is to stand out and inspire your customers to contact you.

For creative Ideas, I would again refer to the success stories you have seen in each section. Or look at those that you encounter in your own life that stand out. See if you can learn anything from what they are doing that you can apply to your business strategy.

5. Measure

Everything today can be measured. Do not let vendors tell you that you cannot connect one medium to another. We have shared ideas of how to do that in this book. Get your vendors to speak in a language you understand.

Give your marketing time but do not fail to adapt if something is not working. A/B test as we discussed.

Remember that your marketing budget is not insignificant and if it is not connected, you are losing on your overall ROI.

A final word.

Now it is time for you to take action. We as authors of this book hope you have been educated on exactly what each of the medias has to offer and a better understanding of how they need to be connected in order for you to maximize your marketing efforts.

So go forth and utilize a Connected Marketing Strategy. Unlock its Power and we wish you nothing but success.

About the Author
Glenn Pasch

As the CEO of PCG Companies, Glenn works with clients to develop new marketing and training strategies that will enable their businesses to become more visible, efficient and profitable.

He continues to author articles for multiple industry publications as well as continuing writing for his blog www.glennpasch. com. He is co-author of the book, "Selling Cars in the Digital Age" which has been translated into 4 languages.

As a highly requested speaker Glenn has been asked to help educate audiences throughout the US and Internationally.

"My passion is helping to create excellent customer experiences and helping teams and individuals to achieve their personal levels of success"

Glenn is a member of The Association for Talent Development as well as the National Speakers Association.

You can contact Glenn at www.pcgcompanies.com

About the Author
Tracy Myers

Tracy is an award-winning small business marketing and branding solutions specialist, car dealership owner, best-selling author, Emmy-winning movie producer, nationally recognized television personality, speaker, business coach, wrestling promoter, and entrepreneur. He is commonly referred to as the Nation's Premier Automotive Solutions Provider while best-selling author and legendary speaker Brian Tracy called him "a visionary . . . a Walt Disney for a new generation." Tracy spends his spare time with charities that are close to his heart and has made his home in Lewisville, North Carolina, with his wife, Lorna, and their two children, Presley and Maddie.

About the Author
Troy Spring

Troy Spring is the CEO of Dealer World, a full-service advertising and consulting agency located in Lehighton, Pennsylvania. His roots in advertising started while he managed four automotive dealerships and the large advertising budgets for the stores. The dealerships all grew under his watch. He credits much of that growth to the advertising decisions he made to drive more business to each location.

He has spent the last decade perfecting what he calls the four pillars of advertising: reach, frequency, creative, and cost. He is a strong advocate of this formula. He spends much of his time sharing these concepts as a national speaker and occasional guest on podcasts, such as *Auto Success Magazine*, *CBT News*, *The Dealer Playbook*, and others, within the industry.

With two best-selling books to his credit, coauthor of *Unfair Advantage* in 2012, and his own motivational book *Turbo Charge Your Life*, he lives in Lehighton, Pennsylvania, with his wife and family. Troy enjoys golf, tennis, and being with family when not working.

Resources:

Gary Vaynerchuk: Jab, Jab Right Hook
Guy Kawasaki: The Art of Social Media
Glenn Pasch: Selling Cars in the Digital Age:
PCG Online Marketing Workshops: www.pcgtraining.com
"Mastering Automotive Digital Marketing" by Brian Pasch
Brightlocal Customer Survey www.brightlocal.com